THE END OF LIFE AS WE KNOW IT

BURIED
TOO MUCH GARBAGE

KATHLYN GAY

Enslow
PUBLISHING

Published in 2016 by Enslow Publishing, LLC
2544 Clinton Street Buffalo, NY 14224

Library of Congress Cataloging-in-Publication Data

Names: Gay, Kathlyn.
Title: Buried: too much garbage / Kathlyn Gay.
Description: New York : Enslow Publishing, 2016. | Series: The end of life as we know it | Includes index.
Identifiers: ISBN 9780766072763 (library bound)
Subjects: LCSH: Refuse and refuse disposal--Juvenile literature. | Waste minimization--Juvenile literature.
Classification: LCC TD792.G39 2016 | DDC 628.4'4--dc23

Printed in the United States of America

To Our Readers: We have done our best to make sure all website addresses in this book were active and appropriate when we went to press. However, the author and the publisher have no control over and assume no liability for the material available on those websites or on any websites they may link to. Any comments or suggestions can be sent by e-mail to customerservice@enslow.com.

Portions of this book originally appeared in the book *Garbage and Recycling.*

Photo Credits: Cover, kanvag/Shutterstock.com; p. 4 kanvag/Shutterstock.com; p. 8 Gregory Adams/Moment Mobile/Getty Images; p. 12 iStock.com/@pixinoo; p.14 Alis Photo/Shutterstock. com; p. 16 Harry Hamburg/New York Daily News Archive/Getty Images; p. 19 Photofusion/Universal Images Group/Getty Images; p. 21 Evan Lorne/Shutterstock.com; p. 24 LI CHAOSHU/Shutterstock. com; p. 28 Studio_G/Shutterstock.com; p. 31 Huguette Roe/Shutterstock.com; p. 33 Radu Bercan/Shutterstock.com; p. 36 Art Konovalov/Shutterstock.com; p. 38 haak78/Shutterstock.com; p. 41 Keystone/Hulton Archive/Getty Images; p. 46 John Patriquin/Portland Press Herald/Getty Images; p. 50 Paul Lesser/Shutterstock.com; p. 53 Bernard Weil/Toronto Star/Getty Images; p. 55 Geography Photos/Universal Images Group/Getty Images; p. 59 Budimir Jevtic/Shutterstock.com; p. 62 Keattikorn/Shutterstock.com; p. 64 Tom Grundy/Shutterstock.com; pp. 66, 73, 78, 95, 99, 103, 117 © AP Images; p. 76 HoleInTheBox/Shutterstock.com; p. 82 BORIS HORVAT/AFP/Getty Images; p. 87 Marvin Joseph/The Washington Post/Getty Images; p. 89 Geo-grafika/Shutterstock.com; p. 92 Petr Student/Shutterstock.com; p. 108 Andrew Burton/Getty Images News/Getty Images; p. 111 Oliver StreweMoment Mobile/Getty Images.

CONTENTS

When you throw out garbage, it does not just disappear. We are facing a worldwide crisis when it comes to garbage and all kinds of waste.

CHAPTER 1

"OUT OF SIGHT, OUT OF MIND"

YOU'VE PROBABLY HEARD OR READ THIS OLD SAYING: "Out of sight, out of mind." It often means that if you don't see a person for a long time, you don't remember him or her. The adage also applies to things—especially things such as garbage and other throwaways. When most people toss out leftover food, they seldom think about what happens to it. It's out of sight, so they forget about it. The same can be said about other kinds of trash.

We not only dispose of food scraps, but also everyday items such as product packaging, grass clippings, furniture, clothing, bottles, newspapers, appliances, paint, and batteries. In addition, there is waste from industries, agriculture, construction, businesses, hospitals, schools, government institutions, parks, and many other sources. In other words, Americans—and people worldwide—are overwhelmed with throwaways, which has created huge problems.

A GARBAGE EXPERIMENT

To create awareness of how individuals contribute to the garbage crisis, some students collect trash that they have generated over a week while in their classroom, cafeteria, shop, art room, and gym. When the trash is dumped out on the classroom floor, it is dramatically apparent that garbage left to pile up would fill the room within a few weeks.

Why should we care what happens to the materials we throw away? Waste that is disposed of improperly can cause pollution. A polluted environment, in turn, can result in a multitude of problems that include harming wildlife and causing disease. Beyond that, garbage and trash contribute to global warming and climate change, according to many political, religious, environmental, and government officials. Yet another related problem that the public seldom recognizes is national and international security. Here is how the Center for Climate and Security in Washington, DC, explained the threats:

> Climate change has a direct impact on security through its effect on the critical infrastructure underpinning a nation's security. This includes sea level rise risks to military installations that can degrade a nation's ability to conduct military operations, as well as extreme weather events that can devastate essential energy, financial and agricultural centers....
>
> Climate change also presents an indirect threat to security by increasing stresses on the critical resources . . . [such as] water, food and energy. These stresses can degrade a

> nation's capacity to govern. Decreases in water, food and energy availability can devastate livelihoods, and contribute to a broad range of destabilizing trends, including internal population displacements and migrations, and political unrest. These pressures in turn can contribute to . . . internal conflict and potentially [a nation's] collapse.[1]

WASTE DISPOSAL

Few places are able to escape the problem of waste disposal. Garbage chokes waterways in many nations. Hikers and bikers trash mountainsides in remote areas such as the Alaskan wilderness and the Himalayas in India and Tibet. Industries generate tons of waste daily, much of which is hazardous. Biomedical waste from hospitals and other healthcare facilities can contaminate the earth and could cause infections or diseases.

Electronics present their own kind of problem. Consider mobile devices from cell phones to laptops to tablets. In late 2014, the number of mobile devices worldwide totaled 7.22 billion, according to an organization known as Groupe Speciale Mobile Association (GMSA), which analyzes mobile electronic data.[2] The number of devices is increasing daily and overtaking the population of the world, which totals between 7.19 and 7.2 billion people. As new electronics are produced, older ones are discarded. "Americans replace their phones every 18 months. Europeans upgrade almost annually," according to the authors of a 2014 report on Cracked.com. The report continues:

> And neither of them holds a candle to Japan, where it takes just nine months for a person to deem their handheld supercomputer so arcane and primitive that it may as well

> have a cord and a crank start. Similar stats exist for laptops and tablets, which is great news for the companies literally telling us to destroy our phones and laptops so we can justify buying shinier ones . . . But you know who doesn't think it's such great news? Mother Nature.

The report points out that these electronic throwaways contain hazardous materials that can leak into the soil and water. In China, for example, "Improper disposal of handheld electronics has already tainted countless

Outdated computers are being thrown away at a high rate which is creating health and environmental issues.

tons of rice with cadmium, chronic exposure to which causes kidney, liver, and lung failure. And cancer. And osteoporosis. The list goes on and on."[3]

Each kind of waste requires a specific method of disposal and treatment. But first take a look at the kind of waste that everyone generates—garbage.

TAKE ACTION!

Make a list of all the food scraps and other items that you throw away during one day. Research how you could reduce those throwaways.

MOUNTAINS OF GARBAGE

On average, each person in the United States throws away 4.38 pounds of solid waste—garbage and other trash—every day. For more than thirty years, the US Environmental Protection Agency (EPA) has collected and reported on Municipal Solid Waste (MSW), the term the agency uses for garbage and trash. The EPA reported that Americans generated about 251 million tons of MSW in 2012, the most recent available data. The EPA noted that organic materials such as paper and paperboard make up 27 percent of MSW, while yard trimmings and food waste are another 28 percent. Plastics account for 13 percent, metals for 9 percent, and rubber, leather, and textiles make up another 9 percent of MSW. Wood comes in at more than 6 percent and glass at almost 5 percent. Miscellaneous wastes make up about 3 percent of the MSW in 2012.[4]

About 54 percent of garbage and other trash goes to landfills. A landfill usually begins as an excavated area or pit. Garbage is dumped in the pit and covered over with a layer of soil. Bacteria in the soil can biodegrade,

Total MSW Generation (by material), 2012
251 Million Tons (before recycling)

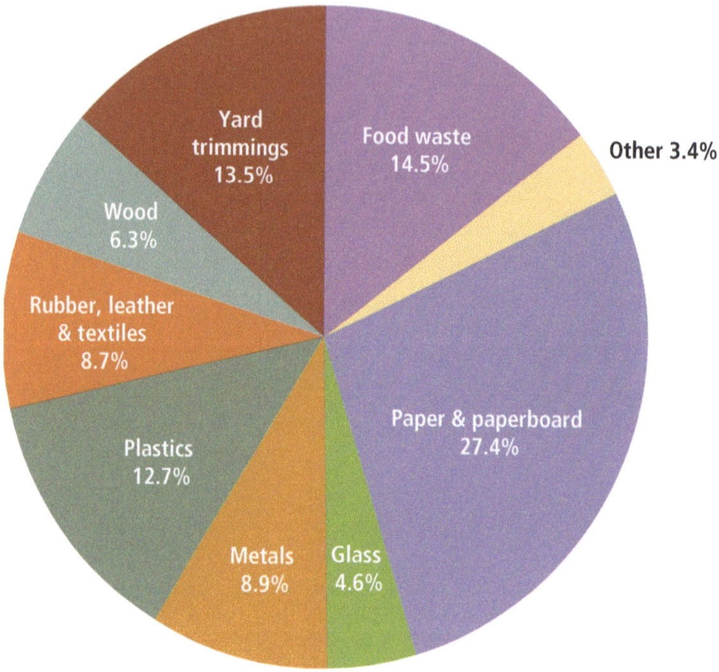

Source: "Municipal Solid Waste Generation, Recycling, and Disposal in the United States: Facts and Figures for 2012," Environmental Protection Agency.

or break down, materials such as food scraps in a relatively short time. Decomposed materials then become part of the earth. But bacteria need oxygen and water to work efficiently. At most modern landfills, machines crush and compact refuse, then each day cover it with earth and pack it down. Layer after layer of trash builds up. Thus the rate of decomposition slows down, and refuse may stay intact for months or many years.

There are varied estimates on how long it takes for items to decompose. Newspapers can stay around for years, aluminum cans take from two hundred to five hundred years to decompose, and some glass and plastics may last millions of years.

TAKE ACTION!

Help reduce plastic water bottles in landfills. Carry your water in a reusable container.

Not only do these materials add to the heaps of waste that fill up disposal sites, but an increasing amount of trash contains toxic substances, such as weed and pest killers, cleaning fluids, paint strippers, and used car oil. Some throwaways contain heavy metals such as lead and mercury which are proven health hazards. Lead may seep from corroding batteries, for example. Children exposed to low levels of lead can suffer brain damage, nervous system disorders, and other developmental problems.

Toxic compounds become part of the leachate, the liquid that percolates through or seeps from solid waste as it decomposes. If a landfill is not properly designed, leachate can run off into streams or seep through the soil into groundwater, the source of drinking water for at least half of the US population. This is a particular concern in areas where there are high levels of precipitation and soils are sandy and porous.

Gases that are generated when solid waste decomposes also are problematic. One of those gases is methane. Methane is generated in landfills as waste decomposes, as well as in the treatment of wastewater. Landfills are the third largest source of methane emissions in the United States, according to the EPA. Methane that discharges into the atmosphere adds to greenhouse gases—the gases that absorb and retain heat from the sun like a hothouse maintains warmth for plants. Carbon dioxide and methane are two important greenhouse gases.

Less than 1 percent of our atmosphere is carbon dioxide, but it is still essential to life on Earth. Plants and trees take in carbon dioxide. They use the carbon to generate new cells and expel the oxygen back into the air, and this becomes the oxygen we breathe. However, our cars, homes, and industries have all caused a huge increase in the amount of carbon dioxide and other greenhouse gases in the atmosphere over the past hundred years or so. This change threatens to disrupt the diversity of habitats and the life dependent on them. A rise of only a few degrees in the earth's average temperature could result in more frequent and intense storms, more rain and flooding in some areas, and droughts in other places.

Although carbon dioxide is the primary greenhouse gas, methane "is the second most prevalent greenhouse gas emitted in the United States from human activities. In 2013, methane accounted for about

The glass of a greenhouse retains heat from the sun to help plants grow. In the same way, the gases in our atmosphere keep the earth warmer than it would otherwise be.

10 percent of all US greenhouse gas emissions from human activities," the EPA reported.[5]

As of August 2013, twenty-nine states had reduced or set targets for limiting greenhouse gas emissions. Statewide targets for reducing emissions are not mandated by law. Rather, they are commitments by the states to reduce greenhouse gases to a specified level in a certain time frame (for example, reducing emissions to 1990 levels by 2020). Some states may implement regulations for emission of greenhouse gases within a certain time frame, and may establish authority for monitoring and enforcing compliance.[6]

PAST GARBAGE DISPOSAL

In the past, rural communities in the United States got rid of their garbage by tossing it into a river and letting the water carry the refuse downstream. Sometimes pigs roamed about consuming garbage. As urban areas developed, people threw their trash into an open dump at the edge of town. These dump sites attracted rats, insects, and other pests, and eventually towns banned the sites. Currently municipal or private trash collectors haul garbage away and usually dispose of it in a landfill or burn it in an incinerator.

MODERN LANDFILLS

In 1976, the US Congress passed the Resource Conservation Recovery Act, which has been amended several times since. Basically, the federal law requires states to construct safe landfills. New ones must be underlined with thick layers of clay, vinyl materials, or both so that leachate will not percolate through the soil.

Water pollution has become a big problem thanks to the common practice of dumping garbage in rivers.

"Modern landfills are well-engineered facilities that are located, designed, operated, and monitored to ensure compliance with federal regulations," the EPA states. "Solid waste landfills must be designed to protect the environment from contaminants which may be present in the solid waste stream." Monitoring systems at the landfill provide safeguards to detect signs of groundwater contamination or gas leakage. "In addition, many new landfills collect potentially harmful landfill gas emissions and convert the gas into energy."[7]

Because of more strict standards for municipal landfills and the high cost of developing new ones, many communities have had to close their older waste disposal sites. Some towns simply do not have a landfill. As a result, municipal and private haulers have to transport trash to sites miles away or across state lines. New York, Maryland, Massachusetts, Ohio, and North Carolina are top exporters of trash out of their states.

North Carolina, for example, has landfills that have the capacity to accept trash until at least 2025, but that is because the state ships the majority of its garbage elsewhere. "From July 2013 to July 2014 North Carolina exported 580,000 tons of waste (primarily to South Carolina, Tennessee, Virginia, and Georgia)," wrote Diane Cherry for North Carolina State University's Institute for Emerging Issues. The state also imported trash, which seems illogical. But, as the report explained, importing trash can be an "economic windfall." An example is the neighboring state of South Carolina, which "has room for 130 million tons of waste; at the rate of $35 per ton, that's a $4.5 billion economic development opportunity."[8]

A BARGE GONE WRONG

Years ago, one trash hauler in New York thought he had discovered an economical way to dispose of waste. In March 1987, he loaded 3,100 tons of garbage from Islip, New York, on a barge and planned to ship it to a site in North Carolina, where the garbage would be converted to methane gas. But the hauler had not obtained approval from North Carolina. State officials suspected the garbage might contain hazardous materials and would not allow the New York barge to unload its cargo.

This barge sailed along the coast of the United States, Mexico, and the Bahamas unable to find anyone willing to take the garbage. Eventually it was burned in New York.

The barge traveled from port to port along US coasts and even to Mexico and the Bahamas. Nobody would allow the garbage to be unloaded. After twenty-three weeks, the barge returned to New York harbor, where the stuff, which was reeking and covered with flies, was finally burned in a Brooklyn incinerator. The ash was buried in an Islip landfill, but not before the material was inspected and found free of hazardous materials.

CHAPTER 2

WHO RECYCLES

SEPARATING MATERIALS—PAPER, METALS, PLASTICS, and so forth—is one of the first steps in recycling. After that, collected materials have to be processed further. Depending on the type of materials, they are cut up, shredded, or prepared in some way for shipment then fabricated or reused in another manufacturing process to make finished goods. Thus, if a new product, such as a bicycle, contains materials that have been reused, only then has recycling in its true sense been accomplished.

To recycle materials such as paper, glass, metals, and fabrics, processing and manufacturing industries must be willing to use throwaways or scrap materials. Consumers must be willing to buy and use products made from recyclables. In other words, there must be a dependable demand for recyclables in both industrial and consumer markets.

The scrap processing industry, which has been involved for more than one hundred years in recycling metals, repeatedly emphasizes that collecting scrap materials is not the same as creating a demand for them. Scrap users, namely manufacturing industries, do not buy scrap materials

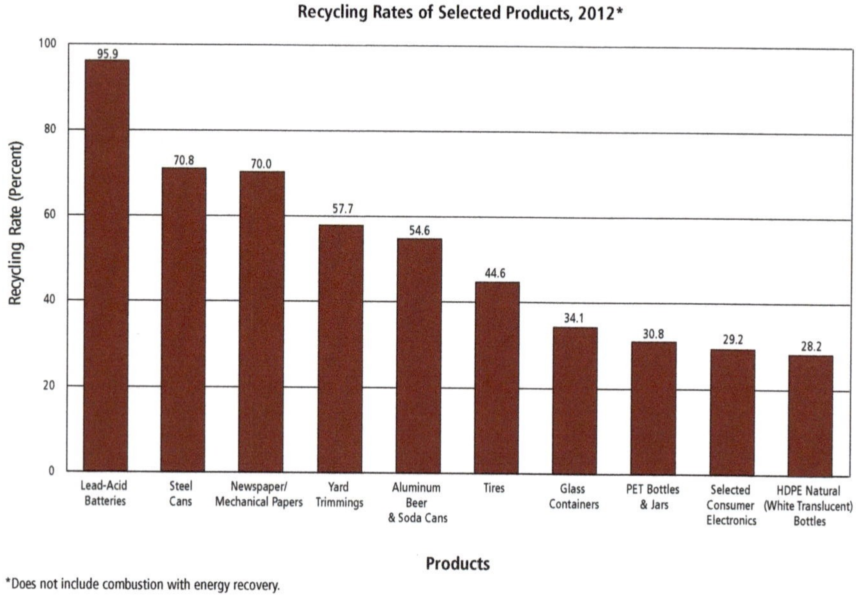

Source: "Municipal Solid Waste Generation, Recycling, and Disposal in the United States: Facts and Figures for 2012," Environmental Protection Agency.

simply because they are available. They must have a use for them, which is generated by demand for their finished products.

Demand, however, can be unpredictable and seesaw up then down again. That has been the case with paper recycling. Supply and demand for recycled paper fluctuates depending on the markets and economic conditions. As various nations improve their economies, demand for recycled paper increases. In 2014. Resource Information Systems, Inc., (RISI) forecast global demand for recycled paper to increase 2.5 percent each year until 2029. Nations with emerging economies are expected to fuel the demand, and countries such as the United States are expected to fulfill the need, which increases income for processors, shippers, and other businesses.[1] Sometimes there is not a large supply of paper goods to recycle. So increasing paper collection not only helps the US economy, but it also helps reduce throwaways that pile up in landfills.

Whatever the benefits of recycling paper or any other product, little is accomplished to protect the earth and reduce climate change if we keep buying things to use up and throw away. As the recycling slogan goes, Reduce, Reuse, Recycle. This suggests that reduction should be the priority. Yet manufacturers, advertisers, marketers, and other sellers constantly urge people to consume—buy more. Consuming more and more is supposed to be a boon to our economy. But if we buy things and soon throw them away, we are back to square one—buried in garbage.

COLLECTING RECYCLABLES

Along with paper, other recyclable materials, such as used glass bottles and jars, aluminum cans, scrap iron and steel products, and some used plastics and fabrics, are also in demand. These recyclables are being

Recycling paper is extremely important for the environment. But it is also crucial that we stop buying so much and start taking steps to reduce the amount of waste we produce.

collected in communities across the United States and in other industrialized nations. An increasing number of voluntary groups are involved in efforts to collect and separate throwaways and send them on to brokers or collection centers. Some of the programs have been started by youth groups, such as 4-H, Boy Scouts, and Girl Scouts, or civic organizations, such as the Jaycees. Chapters of environmental organizations also help set up collection centers for recyclables.

TAKE ACTION!

Ask your classmates, teachers, friends, or relatives to help you set up a large container to collect recyclable glass bottles or aluminum cans at ball games or other outdoor events.

A number of states have organized educational programs that explain the need for recycling. Many of these programs are designed for school classroom use. Schools collect newsprint, cardboard, and white and colored school paper for recycling. Many classrooms have recycling boxes for paper. In one school alone, the students collect enough paper materials to fill four fifty-gallon containers each week. "We don't have to wait until we are older and out of school to take some action to help protect our environment," said one middle school student.

Collecting recyclables is not the only goal of school programs. Usually the purpose of a recycling effort is more broadly based points out the importance of conserving and reusing the Earth's resources and the variety of ways in which this can be done. Some projects include hands-on experience, such as creating artistic drawings or origami—paper folding art—from recycled materials.

In some classrooms, students learn about composting, a form of recycling that creates ideal conditions for household wastes to decompose. Some states have a department of natural resources that provides guidelines for school classes that want to create mini compost piles—indoors in fish aquariums or outdoors in small fenced areas of schoolyards. Students can see biodegradable materials, such as food scraps, leaves, grass clippings, and wood shavings, break down in soil. The humus, or soil from decayed organic matter, that remains can be used again by plants and animals. Such an experiment is an opportunity to learn about other benefits of composting. Because they are not throwing away as much, citizens can save on costs for plastic bags, and cities can cut back on their trash collection costs.

Starting a compost bin in your garden is an easy and effective way to reduce the amount of garbage you throw away.

MUNICIPAL RECYCLING PROGRAMS

Many cities and towns across the United States have established recycling programs operated by municipal sanitation or waste management departments. Some cities have passed laws requiring households and businesses to recycle and have set up facilities for collection or recyclable pickups. In other words, municipal trucks pick up recyclable materials from the curbside once or twice a month at no charge. Or individuals and volunteer groups can take their recyclables to a collection center for aluminum cans, glass jars and bottles, and paper.

Seattle, Washington, has one of the most successful recycling programs in the nation. Residents recycle almost all of their throwaways. In 2011, Seattle's city council called for zero net greenhouse gas emissions by 2050. Half of these emissions come from everyday activities, such as traveling around the city and buying things.

As part of this effort, households put out three types of containers for city waste haulers to collect. CityNext.org, a nonprofit organization that inspires social, economic, and environmental change in cities, explained that residential green containers "hold compost—leftover food and yard clippings. The blue ones overflow with everything recyclable: glass, plastic containers, cans and aluminum foil. The round black ones" are for trash. Food waste goes to a contractor for composting. In September 2014, the city voted to impose fines on residents who do not compost food waste.

All of this recycling has removed hundreds of thousands of metric tons of carbon dioxide from the atmosphere. But as Christine Woodside reported for CityNext.org:

> Of course, even waste-savvy Seattle will not recycle many things that are part of modern American life: prescription

> pill bottles (the plastic is too brittle), wet or dirty produce bags, kitty litter, corks . . . painted wood, treated wood, fats, cooking oils, grease. But officials are working on changing these gaps in its program.

The city expects to collect home cooking oil waste and also separately collect pet waste and diapers in the near future. In addition, efforts are underway to cut greenhouse gas emissions from transportation and commercial buildings.[2]

San Francisco, California, and Portland, Oregon, are two other cities that have exceptional recycling programs, which include collecting organic materials, such as food scraps and yard waste for composting. Many other cities and towns are in the experimental stages with recycling programs operated by municipal sanitation or waste management departments. Some communities have drop-off centers where residents can dispose of their recyclables. Various states have passed laws requiring residents to recycle, and some cities require commercial recycling.

TAKE ACTION!

Organize a group to pick up litter along a roadway or waterway and take the trash to a recycling center.

Once recyclables are collected, they have to be taken to a center where they are sorted for processing. The most common materials collected are paper, glass, and aluminum cans. These materials must be prepared for shipment to a processor or manufacturer who will use them as raw materials for new products.

A paper mill such as this one may reuse materials to make new paper. The used paper must go through a process in which it is treated, washed, and any ink is removed. The paper then must be ground into a pulp before it can be made into new paper.

CHAPTER 3

PROCESSING RECYCLABLES

ONE OF THE MOST FAMILIAR THROWAWAYS IS PAPER. It litters streets, highways, yards, fields, and parking lots. Americans use and throw away tons of paper and paperboard, or cardboard, each year. Of the total 251 million tons of municipal waste generated in the United States, 27.4 percent is paper and paperboard. One source of waste paper is newspapers. Another is office paper. Supermarkets, department stores, and factories throughout the United States also generate tons of paper and paperboard—that is, corrugated or cardboard boxes.

If it has not already been sorted, the paper must be separated into newsprint, corrugated products, and office papers. Each kind of paper may be baled and then shipped by truck or rail to mills. Paper mill workers store the bales in a warehouse until a mill needs the recovered paper.

MADE IN AMERICA

Papermaking began in America as a recycling industry. Until 1860, paper was made primarily from cloth fibers—linen and cotton rags—as well as some wastepaper. With the increasing demand for paper over the next century and with new technology for using wood fibers, most mills phased out their use of rags. A few mills, however, continued to use cotton clippings from textile plants to make high-quality paper for writing and printing. As of 2014, there were 450 paper and pulp mills in the United States and Canada, RISI reported.[1]

Some mills use both recycled paper and wood fiber to make new paper. Recovered paper must be clean and free of food, metal, and other contaminants. These mills are typically set up to process wood fiber and recovered paper into pulp.

Trees for papermaking are cut, and the logs stripped of bark. Then the logs are cut into small chips, which are soaked and cooked with chemicals or ground to a pulp. Usually the pulp is further refined by adding chlorine bleach and heating again in a bleaching tower. The pulp mass is spread on a screenlike belt, pressed, dried, and usually finished with a glossy coating made of clay. Then it is wound on rolls. Rolled paper is cut into smaller rolls or sheets for sale to fabricators.

Environmental groups have been highly critical of wood-pulp mills because such papermaking depletes vast forests. For example, if all copies of one Sunday edition of *The New York Times* could be recycled, about seventy-five thousand trees would still be standing, the Worldwatch Institute has estimated. Although trees are a renewable resource, they take years to grow. Cutting down forests also destroys sinks, or holding places, for carbon dioxide, which, as has been noted, is the primary gas responsible for global warming and climate change.

At a wastepaper recycling mill, the process of making paper is somewhat different from that used to process wood pulp. Recycling mills use wastepaper as raw material. The paper is dumped into a machine called a hydrapulper, which is like a huge kitchen blender, and mixed with water to form a slurry. Wastepaper slurry passes over screens that filter out nonfibrous materials, such as glass, metal, plastic, and dirt. Layers of pulp on the screen have to be drained of excess water. Then the sheets pass between steam-heated rollers that dry and sterilize them, and the paper is smoothed and finished.

From a recycling mill, paper goes to fabricators who make newsprint, writing and printing paper, brown paper sacks, toilet and facial tissues, paper towels and napkins, and paperboard used to package a variety of products. Fabricators also use recycled paper pulp to produce insulation materials, molded packaging products—such as egg cartons and flower pots—and shredded material to protect objects that might be damaged when transported.

Still, the demand for recycled paper helps determine how much will be produced. If the demand increases, manufacturers will spend the money for equipment to recycle wastepaper or to build new recycling mills. In some cases, demand can be created through advertising and marketing programs. Consumers concerned about environmental problems often buy products that suggest a manufacturer is recycling or using natural resources wisely. The American Paper Institute encourages manufacturers to use recycled packaging materials for their products and to print the recycling symbol on their packages.

Arrows in the shape of a triangle indicate that a product is recyclable.

GLASS: THE NEVER-ENDING RECYCLABLE

Toss out a glass jar or bottle and it is likely to be around for a million years. But a glass container does not have to be buried alive in a landfill or left as litter. In fact, some states require that consumers pay a deposit on glass bottles so these containers will be returned to stores or collection centers for reuse or recycling.

Glass recycling follows fairly basic steps. Most collection centers accept only glass that has been sorted by color—clear, amber or brown, and green. Metal caps and rings have to be removed, although paper labels can usually stay on the containers. From the collection center, used glass containers are shipped to a glass plant, where machines crush bottles and jars into small pieces called cullet. After the cullet is cleaned, other machines mix it with sand, soda ash, and limestone and then feed the mixture into a hot furnace. Molten, or melted, glass drops into molds, and compressed air blows the glass against the walls of the mold, which forms its shape. Newly formed bottles or jars are reheated and then cooled slowly, a process that prevents shattering.

GLASS RECYCLING STATISTICS

The Glass Packaging Institute publishes statistics about glass recycling on its website. A brief selection of the data are shown here:

- More than a ton of natural resources are saved for every ton of glass recycled.
- One ton of carbon dioxide is reduced for every six tons of recycled glass used in the manufacturing process.
- Manufacturers benefit from recycling in several ways—it reduces emissions and consumption of raw materials, extends the life of plant equipment such as furnaces, and saves energy.
- An estimated 80 percent of all glass containers recovered for recycling are remelted in furnaces and used in the manufacture of new glass containers.[2]

After new glass bottles and jars are used, they can once again be recycled over and over. In fact, glass is 100 percent recyclable. "This means that every pound of glass bottles and jars brought to a recycling center can make a pound of new glass containers," the Glass Container Industry says.

ALUMINUM IS MORE THAN CANS

Mention aluminum and many people think of aluminum beverage cans. When empty cans are thrown away, they total in the billions and add to heaps of garbage and trash. But the good news is that used aluminum beverage cans are the most recycled item in the United States. Who collects all of these cans? Many are individuals—perhaps you are among them—who simply save used aluminum soft drink and beer cans and take them to collection centers or scrap metal yards and sell them.

With mandatory recycling programs in some cities, many households set out aluminum cans for curbside pickup by municipal waste haulers. School groups, civic and religious organizations, job training centers for the handicapped, the poor and homeless, government workers, and employees of a variety of firms collect cans for recycling and the income the cans bring.

Civic groups often use their earnings from cans to pay for special needs. One school in Utah used funds from its can recycling program to buy a public address system for its football stadium, while students in New Hampshire bought computers with recycling funds. Neighborhood associations raise money through aluminum can recycling programs to improve their local parks. Zoos, animal care clinics, and humane shelters have benefited from can recycling programs.

Bales of crushed aluminum cans await recycling. It takes much less energy to recycle used cans than it does to create the metal for new cans.

Alcoa, a major aluminum manufacturer, has established Alcoa Recycling, which helps groups and communities across the nation set up aluminum can recycling programs. The company provides a packet of free materials that includes a guide for equipping and publicizing an aluminum can recycling effort.

Turning cans into cash motivates most people who recycle aluminum cans. It also helps the environment. The most obvious benefit of aluminum recycling is pulling cans from the solid waste stream and easing the load on landfills. Recycling also saves energy. Aluminum is made from bauxite ore, and 7.5 kilowatt hours of electricity are needed to produce each pound of metal from the ore. According to Alcoa, "For each pound of aluminum recycled, Americans save the energy resources needed to generate about 7 kilowatt hours of electricity—enough to power the average home for six hours."[3]

In addition to aluminum beverage cans, "other types of aluminum, such as siding, gutters, car components, storm window frames and lawn furniture can also be recycled," states Elgin Recycling, a private company based in Elgin, Illinois. According to the company:

- Recycling one aluminum can saves enough energy to run a TV for three hours or the equivalent of a half a gallon of gasoline.
- Because so many of them are recycled, aluminum cans account for less than 1 percent of the total US waste stream, according to EPA estimates.
- An aluminum can that is thrown away will still be a can five hundred years from now.
- There is no limit to the amount of times an aluminum can may be recycled.
- We use more than eighty billion aluminum soda cans every year.
- Americans throw away enough aluminum every month to rebuild our entire commercial air fleet.

KICKING THE CAN DOWN THE ROAD

While kicking a can down a street or alley has long been a diversion for some young people, it is also sometimes the case in politics. However, a legislator or other government official does not literally kick a can. Rather, the phrase kicking the can down the road is an idiom that means delaying a decision in hopes that the problem or issue will go away or somebody else will deal with it later. Do you think that applies to the problem of global warming?

Steel cans are used for a variety of food items and are 100 percent recyclable.

- An estimated eighty million Hershey's Kisses are wrapped each day, which uses enough aluminum foil to cover more than fifty acres of space. All that foil is recyclable but not many people realize it.[4]

STEEL CANS

Steel cans also are part of the trash heap in most areas of the world. The tin-plated steel can has been used since 1820 to store and preserve foods and beverages. In the past, all steel cans were welded together, so liquids sometimes leaked from the seams. Steel cans were also heavy and tended to give drinks a metallic taste. Thus when seamless, lightweight aluminum beverage cans were first produced in the 1960s, they became the primary packaging choice for beverage companies.

Food products, however, are still packed in regular seamed steel cans for the most part. So are some coffee and pet food products. Steel is one of the most recycled materials in the United States, and it is a part of many curbside and drop-off collection programs. However, don't expect to earn much cash by collecting and selling steel cans. Steel is a scrap metal, and a large amount has to be collected before it is worth much.

Used steel containers of all types, like other throwaways, become part of the solid waste stream. When steel cans are sorted out of waste, they are sent to recyclers. The steel industry has long been involved in the reuse of scrap metals and has actively sought ways to inform the public about steel can recycling. The Can Manufacturers Institute, for example, points out that steel cans are 100 percent recyclable and that recycling one ton of steel cans saves 2,500 pounds of iron ore, 1,400 pounds of coal, and 120 pounds of limestone, which are the raw ingredients for making steel.[5] After steel cans are collected and recycled, they are used to make new food cans, paint cans, aerosol cans, and other materials.

EXAMPLES OF PRODUCTS MADE FROM RECYCLABLES

- Recycled office paper may become notebook paper, napkins, paper towels, or toilet paper.
- Recycled newspapers may become kitty litter, paper plates, or egg cartons.
- Recycled glass jars and bottles may become new jars and bottles or fiberglass.
- Recycled plastic beverage bottles may become backpacks, sleeping bags, or carpets.
- Recycled steel cans may become parts for bikes and cars, new steel cans, or steel beams.
- Recycled aluminum cans become new aluminum cans.

CHAPTER 4

METAL MINES ABOVE GROUND

IN NUMEROUS US CITIES AND TOWNS, HOUSEHOLDS and businesses regularly dispose of metal throwaways along with their garbage that trash collectors pick up. In some communities there are spring or fall clean-up days for haulers to pick up what most people refer to as junk—rusty tools, broken bicycles, old bed springs, and countless other items. But what if discarded metal goods from households and waste metal materials from industry and businesses were simply left to pile up for months?

In just one small factory that manufactures metal products, trim from stamping machines can fill up collection bins in a matter of hours. Within months, the bins would fill up many times. Multiply that by thousands of factories that generate scrap metal materials. Then add scrap from bridges and buildings that have been torn down and thousands of junk cars left on streets, alleys, or vacant lots each year. As you can imagine, if the scrap metals generated in major cities and

Every year thousands of old vehicles are abandoned by their owners. These cars and trucks must then be collected by the city or town to be recycled as scrap metal.

towns were not picked up and recycled on a regular basis, a mountain of scrap would be created.

Fortunately, the scenario described is not likely to occur since scrap metal is collected in cities across the nation and processed for reuse. In fact, throughout history, wherever and whenever scrap metals have been generated, they have been recycled.

AN OLD PRACTICE

Scrap metal recycling is an ancient practice. In times of war, farmers in ages past often converted their plows and other tools into swords and spears. Conquering armies tore down metal statues and ornaments to melt them down into armor, weapons, household items, or other objects. Throughout Europe, scrap iron dealers have collected and processed scrap iron and other metals for centuries. During America's revolution, the colonists collected their copper and iron pots and metal utensils, and deposited them in the town square. The metal goods were melted down to make weapons.

In the more recent past, scrap metal recycling was an important part of the Industrial Revolution. Immigrant peddlers of the late 1800s and early 1900s earned a living by collecting rags and old iron in horse-drawn wagons. Some of these peddlers began scrap metal yards and collected large amounts of scrap to process for resale and reuse in mills.

Many family-owned scrap yards began operations in the late 1800s. These early scrap processors usually had only hand tools, such as sledgehammers and chisels, to help them break up large metal objects. It was hard, dirty, unglamorous work. Even after the turn of the century, when huge machines became available, only a few scrap processors could afford to make a large investment in crushers, shredders, and balers.

Still, as more and more large scrap yards with modern equipment opened up, smaller family firms kept operating, too. Both the family and national companies were vital in providing the raw materials needed to produce military equipment during World War II.

OUTDOOR FACTORIES

Most family-owned scrap yards today have machinery to process the heavy stuff. In fact, a scrap yard dealer, whether the owner of a small business or part of a huge national or international company, runs a factory without a roof—a place where raw materials are processed. You can find a scrap metal yard in or on the outskirts of almost every city in the United States.

When scrap metals come into a scrap yard, they must be sorted first into ferrous metals, or scrap that contains iron and steel, nonferrous materials, such as aluminum, copper, and lead, and precious metals, such as gold and silver.

Ferrous scrap is by far the largest amount of material processed by a scrap yard, and it comes in the form of obsolete scrap—the type picked up from households. Another major source of ferrous scrap is manufacturing plants that generate leftover materials, such as the scrap that comes from holes drilled into steel sheets to make auto parts. Steel mills also create scrap after forming raw steel into bars, sheets, and other shapes. All three categories of scrap materials must be further sorted into dozens of different grades and sizes that steel mills and foundries will use once again.

The old cars in this scrap yard have been gutted and pressed into small bundles.

Huge machines in scrap yards slice, smash, pound, shred, and bale everything from automobile hulks to steel girders from buildings. If a car ends up in a scrap yard, tires, seats, window glass, battery, radiator, and most other parts are removed. A crane then picks up the hulk and drops it into the bin of a hydraulic press, or baler. With thousands of pounds of pressure, the baler squeezes the car hulk into a compact bundle about the size of a large TV set.

In some scrap yards, car hulks are shredded on a huge machine that looks somewhat like a roller coaster. A crane picks up one carcass at a time from a mountain of car hulks in the yard. As each one is dropped onto the shredder, it is ripped apart in seconds. Steel hammers break through the shell the way a comb rakes through a thick head of hair. The fist-sized pieces then pass over magnetic drums that separate iron and steel from other metals and nonmetallic materials, such as glass and plastic. The shredded pieces pile up on the ground at the end of a chute and are eventually loaded onto a freight car or truck—ready for shipment to a steel mill.

Scrap steel is now essential in steel manufacturing. In the past, nearly all steelmaking required virgin iron ore mined and shipped to mills, where it was melted down with coal, limestone, and scrap metals in basic oxygen furnaces. But now North American steel is always made with "a minimum of 25 percent recycled content," according to the Steel Recycling Institute. The institute explains:

> Steel is continuously recyclable—meaning it can be recycled over and over without loss of quality. . . . Steel is North America's most recycled material with more steel recycled

than paper, plastic, aluminum and glass combined. Through recycling, the steel industry saves the energy equivalent to power 20 million homes for one year.[1]

MAJOR RECYCLABLES

Of the nonferrous scrap collected, aluminum is a major recyclable. "Nearly 75 percent of all aluminum produced in the US is still in use today. Aluminum can be recycled over and over again without any loss to quality. In fact, an aluminum beverage container can be recycled and back on the shelf in 60 days," the Aluminum Association reported.[2]

Scrap yards, like recycling collection centers, usually process aluminum beverage cans. Discarded aluminum lawn chair frames, siding and gutters from buildings, and aluminum scrap from industries such as mobile home and travel trailer manufacturers also are processed in a scrap yard. Aluminum must be crushed and bundled or shredded before it can be shipped to a smelting plant, where it will be melted down to produce new aluminum.

A VITAL WAR PRODUCT

Aluminum foil, a product in high demand today for wrapping foods for refrigeration or storage, was vital to war efforts in the 1940s. American families saved strips of foil, often from gum wrappers, and rolled it into balls to be turned over to US government collection centers. During World War II, the military used aluminum foil to package products and prevent damage by moisture, vermin, and heat. Aluminum also was used for insulation, electrical capacitors, and as radar shields.

Copper is another major metal that is recycled. "Each year in the USA, nearly as much copper is recovered from recycled material as is derived from newly mined ore . . . and when you exclude wire production, most of which uses newly refined copper, the amount of copper used by copper and brass mills, ingot makers, foundries, powder plants and other industries shows that nearly three-fourths (72%) comes from recycled copper scrap," according to the Copper Development Association.[3]

Other metals recovered include lead, primarily from batteries and car radiators, nickel from stainless steel kitchen appliances, and silver from used photographic film.

Young women pull a wheelbarrow full of pots and pans in 1940. The metal was recycled and used for the war effort.

"Is there gold in them thar' hills" of scrap? The question is a common one, and the answer is sometimes. Seldom would gold jewelry or gold coins be found in a scrap yard, but gold can be recovered from various industrial products. Gold is an excellent conductor of electricity, and the metal has been used in computer circuits, telephone systems, and even in high-quality spark plugs. Recovering gold from industrial wastes requires special equipment to flush the precious metal from other materials.

RECYCLING CREATES JOBS

In May 2015, the Institute of Scrap Recycling Industries (ISRI) released an Economic Impact Study showing that the industry accounts for nearly half a million jobs in the United States and generates more than $105 billion annually in economic activity.[4]

Through the efforts of scrap processors, countless throwaways enter the recycling loop and are reused. With all of the metals processed in the scrap industry, it is not surprising that scrap yards are sometimes called metal mines above ground.

BARRIERS TO SCRAP RECYCLING

The scrap industry long has struggled with a variety of complex economic and environmental issues. In some cases, it may cost a steel mill less to use virgin raw materials than to buy scrap, particularly if the steel mill owns and operates iron ore mines. Scrap processors may also have to pay higher rates for transporting scrap metals than mining companies pay to ship ore, coal, and limestone.

TAKE ACTION!

Ask a teacher, school administrator, or environmental group to arrange a classroom trip to a scrap yard to see the piles at the metal mine above ground.

In addition, like most other recyclers, scrap metal dealers cannot set their own prices for the goods they sell. Instead, mills and foundries that buy scrap metals determine what they will pay for the materials they need. For example, let's say a mill usually pays $100 a ton for scrap but a year or two later offers only $50 a ton because the supply has increased. Then when there is little scrap available, a mill might pay well over $100 a ton for scrap. Scrap processors either supply the scrap at the offered price or wait until the price rises.

The scrap metal industry must also deal with manufactured goods that contain hazardous materials. Some examples are household appliances and fluorescent light fixtures that were once manufactured with electrical capacitors containing polychlorinated biphenyls (PCBs), a highly toxic chemical compound in the capacitor fluids. Although the Environmental Protection Agency (EPA) banned PCBs in 1979, regulations did not cover PCBs in discarded appliances and other products. Then in 1988, the EPA determined that smashing and shredding products with PCBs leaves a contaminated residue. As a result, the EPA ruled that if the residue contains more than fifty parts per million of PCBs, it must be buried in a special hazardous waste landfill or incinerated.

Equipment and material manufactured before July 2, 1979 and not marked No PCBs include:

- Automobiles
- Reusable automobile parts
- Transformer shells
- Heat transfer equipment
- Hydraulic equipment
- Electrical equipment parts
- Oil and grease-filled insulated electrical cable
- Hydraulic oil
- Brake fluid
- Recycled oil
- Oil recovered from steam cleaning
- Ignition coil capacitors
- Drums and containers
- Major home appliance capacitors (cylindrical objects usually located near the appliance motor or compressor)
- Fluff (shredder waste from automobiles and appliances).[5]

The PCB regulation means that scrap processors have to pay the costs of transporting and disposing of the residue with the toxic waste. But if processors cannot earn enough from the sale of cut-up scrap appliances to pay the increased handling costs, they may not accept old refrigerators, air conditioners, and other products made with PCBs.

That situation, in turn, creates a ripple effect. Appliance dealers often have trouble selling new products when they cannot help their customers get rid of old ones. If sales fall, dealers may be forced to go out of business, which means losses to manufacturers.

Another environmental problem concerns air bags in automobiles. The US Department of Transportation urged manufacturers to install air bags as safety features—they are designed to inflate on impact, which protects drivers if their cars crash. Sodium azide causes the bags to inflate, but if the chemical is unspent, it can be a health hazard. Not only is sodium azide highly toxic and a suspected carcinogen, or cancer-causing agent, but it is also explosive. In scrap vehicles, air bag cartridges that have not been deployed are hazardous waste unless they are sent to a reclamation facility to be safely recovered. If they are reclaimed, they are not hazardous waste. Air bags that have been deployed are no longer dangerous, and no special precautions are needed.

The Institute of Scrap Recycling Industries, which represents more than sixteen hundred chapters nationwide, has attempted to point out the dangers of manufacturing goods without regard to their afterlife. In other words, the institute hopes that more manufacturers will reduce or eliminate their use of hazardous materials. As has happened in the past, consumers must create a demand for products that will not harm the environment or human health. At the same time, scrap processors would like to see a national policy that promotes the design and manufacture of goods that can be recycled safely and efficiently.

In Portland, Maine, an ecomaine worker sorts through waste on a conveyor belt. Whatever is not recyclable is burned to create fuel.

CHAPTER 5

WASTE BECOMES ENERGY

WASTE-TO-ENERGY **IS A TERM TOSSED ABOUT A LOT** in political discussions, recycling industries, and environmental organizations. The main focus is on how recyclables, from food and yard waste to used motor oil, can be burned to produce energy. Some cities truck all garbage and trash to incinerators and claim that burning refuse is less expensive than landfill disposal. Incinerators prevent hazardous waste materials from seeping into the ground. In addition, burning refuse eliminates large amounts of trash that would otherwise go to a landfill and helps reduce greenhouse gas emissions.

Some incinerators create steam to produce electricity, and the ash contains metals that can be recycled. Consider a waste-to-energy plant called ecomaine in Portland, Maine. The plant "receives trash identified as un-recyclable and converts it at 2000 degrees Fahrenheit to energy in the form of electricity." The waste-to-energy plant "processes about 175,000 tons of trash a year and . . . generates enough steam to create about 100,000 to 110,000 megawatt-hours of electricity annually—enough to power about 14,000 homes for a year." The plant has received a variety of awards, including one from the American Society of Mechanical Engineers for the plant's "innovative and technical contributions to solid waste processing, environmental performance, and health and safety records."[1]

Still, there are disadvantages. Incinerators may emit hazardous greenhouse gases that contribute to climate change. "Environmental groups oppose them, saying that although cleaner than the incinerators of the past, waste-to-energy plants still emit mercury, lead, dioxins and a variety of other toxic substances. And the history of incineration offers a cautionary tale, producing alarm among some who live nearby," according to a feature in the *New York Times*.

In early 2015, a huge waste-to-energy plant started up near West Palm Beach, Florida. Reportedly, it can burn up to three thousand tons of trash daily, which provides electricity for thousands of houses. "Mark Hammond, executive director of the county's Solid Waste Authority, said the incinerator was the best available way to dispose of waste—and a far better solution than placing a new landfill near the Everglades, which was the county's original plan," the *Times* reported.[2] Burning the waste has also reduced greenhouse gas emissions.

EARLY WASTE-TO-ENERGY EFFORTS

In the early 1980s, Portsmouth, New Hampshire, began burning trash to generate steam that produced electricity, which was sold to a nearby military facility. Converting waste to energy was a way for Portsmouth to produce income at a time when federal aid to local and state governments had been cut drastically. News articles called Portsmouth's waste-burning effort "an unusual way to ease the budget strain."

Currently, cities and private businesses across the United States have developed waste-to-energy plants not only to generate cash but also to deal with the garbage disposal crisis. Some municipal incinerators burn all solid waste without sorting or processing, which produces energy in the form of steam that is recovered in a boiler. The steam may be used for industrial purposes, heating buildings, or generating electricity.

Although cities often burned solid waste in the past, most municipal incinerators were shut down after the 1970 Clean Air Act and later amendments banned hazardous pollutants emitted from smokestacks. Emissions from waste burners have polluted the air with sulfur dioxide, nitrogen oxides, and other gases that build up in the atmosphere and trap heat from the Earth, which in turn increases global temperature. Global warming changes climate patterns and landforms worldwide. Sulfur dioxide and nitrogen oxides also are responsible for acid deposition, or acid rain. In the atmosphere, the gases form acidic substances that fall to the Earth in wet or dry form and cause damage to lakes, forests, and some monuments and other structures.

Another major concern about mass burning was that many incinerators released heavy metals and dioxins into the atmosphere. Dioxin compounds, which include seventy-five different species, have been linked to such health problems as birth defects and disorders of the immune system that leave people vulnerable to disease. Some of the most hazardous of the dioxin compounds have been found in emissions from older waste burners and in the remaining ash.

But as more and more municipal landfills have closed, city officials have had to find ways to dispose of waste and have built new mass-burn facilities that turn waste into energy. Like the Florida waste-to-energy plant, others are under construction or in the planning stages. According to one study sponsored by the renewable fuel industry, each ton of solid waste that is burned can produce the amount of electricity a typical residence uses in a month. Manufacturers of new waste burners also argue

This is a poster protesting the use of incinerators to burn waste. The subject is controversial: Critics point to the toxins that are released into the environment. Proponents claim that new technology can keep emissions at an acceptable level.

that air pollution control devices in burners keep toxic emissions within legal limits, and high temperatures destroy waste without producing large volumes of toxic ash.

Nevertheless, critics say that burning waste is not an efficient way to produce energy because of the high costs—hundreds of millions of dollars—of building the plants and installing filters and scrubbers to prevent toxic emissions. In addition, citizens in some communities are still concerned about pollutants and have organized protests to fight the building of new mass-burners or campaigned for strict regulations on operating the burners. Communities have also refused to allow waste incinerator ash to be dumped in landfills.

THE *KHIAN SEAFOR*

Like the garbage from Islip, New York, that nobody wanted, another widely publicized case from the past involved unwanted waste from a Philadelphia incinerator that produced fifteen thousand tons of toxic ash. At the time, there was no place in Philadelphia or nearby areas to dump the ash, so it was loaded on a barge called the *Khian Seafor* to transport to an out-of-state landfill site.

The *Khian Seafor* began its trip in late 1986. But like the barge of Islip garbage, no one wanted the incinerator waste. No port along the Atlantic Coast would allow the *Khian Seafor* unload. The barge traveled to at least eleven other nations, where officials also refused the cargo, although the captain has been accused of dumping two thousand tons of ash on a Haitian beach, which caused environmental hazards. Finally, twenty-seven months later, in November 1988, the ash was dumped into the Indian Ocean. No one knows what effect it had on sea life.

An alternative type of waste-burning technology is to sort materials that will burn from those that are noncombustible. Noncombustibles go to a landfill, and combustible materials are sorted into heavy and light components. The lighter materials are burned as a fuel, known as refuse-derived fuel, to produce energy. Heavier wastes are sorted further to remove glass and metals, then the remaining materials are mixed with wet sludge from sewage treatment plants. The mixture goes to a digester, where it decomposes, becomes humus, which is like compost, and is used to fertilize gardens and lawns.

COMPOSTING

Another method for dealing with solid waste is composting—the process of creating a pile of organic wastes, such as food scraps, leaves, and grass clippings, layering these materials, adding moisture, and aerating, or turning it regularly to provide oxygen. Successful composting depends on adequate levels of moisture, oxygen, bacteria, and heat, all of which help organic materials decay. The end product can be used to fertilize or to help soil retain moisture.

Some midwestern and eastern cities have set up large composting sites for leaves. Huge leaf-loading machines sweep up leaves that have been raked or blown to the curb. The machines dump the leaves in heaps at a land site called a staging area. Tractors break up the leaves, which are watered and formed into six- or seven-foot-high piles known as windrows.

Just before winter, the volume of the windrows has usually shrunk by at least half, and the leaves are turned. The windrows maintain enough heat through the winter to aid in the decay process. In the spring and summer, the windrows are turned again. By the end of the summer, all the windrows are pushed together. The decay process continues until the following spring, when the resulting compost is ready to be used as fertilizer.

Some US cities have developed municipal composting systems to process all or most of their food and yard wastes. Seattle, Washington, and San Francisco, California, are two examples. The cities have curbside programs to collect organic waste for municipal composting. In San Francisco, composting is mandatory. In 2013, the city diverted 80 percent of all its waste to either recycling or composting. The city has set a goal to have no waste of any kind sent to landfills by 2020.[3]

In 2014, New York City's Department of Sanitation (DSNY) was collecting organic waste for composting from 100,000 households and

In Toronto, residents can leave out their Green Bins of organic waste to be picked up along with garbage and other recycling.

some schools. The department expanded their curbside collections of organic waste to a total of at least 135,000 households in 2015. "Organic waste accounts for about 31% of all waste generated by residents in New York City," the DSNY reported. "Organic waste includes yard waste, food scraps, compostable paper (napkins, paper plates, etc.), and other materials suitable for industrial-scale composting."[4]

Some of New York City's public schools are also participating in a municipal composting program. The New York City Department of Education, in a partnership with the DSNY, has set up an Organic Waste Collection Program in the city's schools. "Participating schools have a station of color-coded refuse bins in cafeterias—one for organics, and others for liquids, recycling and landfill. Students are educated to separate their waste accordingly. The organic waste is collected by the city and brought to commercial composting facilities where it is used to create nutrient-rich soil for resale," wrote Chris Nicholson for the district administration in the fall of 2014. The school administration's goal is to get "all of the city's 1,300 public educational facilities included in the waste collection program by the 2016–17 [school] year."[5]

RECYCLING WASTE MOTOR OIL

Oil is a natural resource and a major source of energy for industrialized nations. But seldom do people think about reusing waste motor oil from vehicles. Most vehicle owners take their car, van, or truck to a mechanic or auto repair shop for an oil change. The shop owner or mechanic then disposes of the oil properly for reprocessing.

Used motor oil can be reprocessed into fuel. "It can be burned in furnaces for heat, or in power plants to generate electricity for homes, schools and businesses. Processed motor oil can also be used in industrial burners, or re-refined into high-quality motor oil. Just two gallons of used oil can generate enough electricity to run the average household for almost 24 hours," according to the American Petroleum Institute (API).[6]

Not everyone with a motorized vehicle uses commercial services for oil changes. Some people change their own vehicle oil, and API encourages them to take used oil to a collection center for recycling.

> Used motor oil that is collected by "do-it-yourselfers" is critical to the used oil recycling system. Next time you change your own oil, remember, you can make a difference by recycling the oil from your car, truck, motorcycle, boat, recreational vehicle or lawnmower. By dropping off your

This recycling center in England allows people to drop off aluminum, car batteries, paint, and motor oil in separate bins.

> used motor oil today you help prevent pollution and conserve energy for a safer and healthier tomorrow.[7]

In spite of such advice, some people pour used motor oil on the ground or over a dirt or gravel road to control dust, bury it in a yard, or dump it in a sewer drain. Improper motor oil disposal can create a variety of hazards. It may seep into groundwater supplies, which can contaminate drinking water. Motor oil in sewer systems can disrupt bacteria that break down sewage. Oil in streams and lakes can interfere with the oxygen level in water, which destroys aquatic life. Toxic substances in used oil may accumulate in the tissues of plants and animals that people eat.

CREATING PUBLIC AWARENESS

A major obstacle to recycling used motor oil is the lack of public awareness of the environmental dangers involved in improper dumping. In addition, there is not widespread understanding that used motor oil can be re-refined or used to produce energy. As the petroleum industry has pointed out, if all the used oil generated each year could be burned to generate electricity, the energy needs of hundreds of thousands of homes would be met.

Informing the public about the need for recycling used motor oil is a primary task. For do-it-yourselfers, the next step is locating a place to dispose of used motor oil. One way to find a location is on the website Earth911.com.[8] Just type in your zip code and local businesses or government centers will be listed. For example, the listing could include Auto Zone, Advance Auto Parts, Walmart Tire and Lube Express, Tires Plus, or a hazardous waste facility.

WASTE MOTOR OIL FACTS

According to the Public Works Department of Davis, California:

- Each year, millions of gallons of used oil are illegally poured down drains, sewers, or the trash.
- One gallon of used motor oil can pollute one million gallons of drinking water.
- Used motor oil can be re-refined into new oil that is just as good as new.
- Before it is drained, an oil filter can contain more than a pint of used oil.
- Oil filters containing oil should not be thrown into the trash. Remember to recycle!
- It takes one gallon of used oil to produce 2.5 quarts of re-refined oil.
- If all used motor oil generated by the public was collected and re-refined, it would provide enough oil for more than five million cars each year.
- Extensive laboratory testing and field studies show re-refined oil is equivalent to virgin oil.
- Used oil can contain such contaminants as lead, magnesium, copper, zinc, chromium, arsenic, chlorides, cadmium, and chlorinated compounds. Oil poured down drains, onto the ground, or put in the garbage can work its way into our ground and surface waters and cause serious pollution.[9]

THROWAWAY TIRES

Americans discard an estimated 290 to 300 million tires each year. Although some landfills accept scrap tires, most operators do not want that type of solid waste. Tires are designed to be nearly indestructible and do not compact well because of their air pockets. Unless scrap tires are buried carefully—deep underground and mixed well with other wastes—they will float or rise to the surface.

Tires that come to the surface of a landfill or tires stored above ground present another type of problem: The water that collects in them provides breeding sites for mosquitoes. Scrap tires above ground also may attract rodents that spread disease. In addition, tires are combustible, and if they pile up, they become fire hazards. Sometimes arsonists set fire to piles of tires, which may burn out of control and create heavy smoke pollution. Burning tires also emit significant amounts of carbon dioxide and dioxins, which contribute to greenhouse gases and climate change.

Minnesota was one of the first states to set policies and pass legislation to deal with problems associated with discarded tires. The state banned used tires from landfills in 1985. If tire stockpiles are hazardous to public health, owners must clean up their sites. Currently many other states also prohibit disposal of scrap tires in landfills. So how do consumers, businesses, and governments get rid of these discards?

TAKE ACTION!

Visit an auto repair shop or a business that sells tires and interview the owner to learn how he or she disposes of scrap tires.

Some throwaway tires are reclaimed to produce materials used for paving roads or to manufacture products like floor mats and fencing. Some tire discards are buried on hillsides to prevent erosion. But such applications consume only small quantities of scrap tires. Larger volumes of them are ground to make a pulverized rubber, known as crump rubber, which is combined with binders to produce rubberized sealers and asphalt rubber for highways and athletic surfaces.

"About 130 million tires are used annually as tire-derived fuel (TDF)"—that is, they are burned like other fuel sources, such as coal, according to Marc Lallanilla writing for GreenLiving.about.com.[10] Many US industries across the country use TDF as supplemental fuel to increase boiler efficiency and decrease air emissions. Industries that use TDF include cement kilns, pulp and paper mills, and electric utilities. "More than 52 percent of the 300 million scrap tires generated annually are consumed as TDF in these facilities, providing a cleaner and more economical alternative to traditional fuels," ScrapTireNews.com reported.

Only one facility in the United States is "specifically designed to burn whole tires or tire-derived-fuel as its only fuel." This plant in Sterling, Connecticut, is "a 25-megawatt electric-generating facility . . . and currently

Piles of discarded tires lie next to ones that have been shredded. The disposal of old tires is a challenging one. Tire-derived fuel holds promise, but only one facility in the country is currently designed to burn tires.

consumes nearly 10 million tires annually. Historically, the tires-to-energy plant has achieved emission rates below those at electric generating plants with solid fuel combustors powered by traditional fuels."[11]

In spite of the advantages of this dedicated tire-to-energy facility, "there are no known facilities under construction or consideration," the EPA reported. "The length of time and cost of construction, as well as the deregulation of the utility industry hinders further expansion of this industry."[12]

CHAPTER 6

EXPLOSION OF PLASTICS

ON ALMOST ANY GIVEN DAY, YOU ARE LIKELY TO USE something made of plastic or buy a product packaged in some type of plastic wrap. Plastics are so much a part of our way of life that most people would have difficulty living without them. From bottles and cups to telephones and toothbrushes, plastic goods—perhaps more than any other products—are symbols of a society geared for convenience and consumption without regard to their role in climate change.

The use of plastic helps merchants and manufacturers sell large quantities of goods. In supermarkets and self-service stores, retailers and customers want products that are packaged and ready to take to the check-out counter. Unlike the past, when retail clerks selected the items that customers wanted, today's shoppers usually make their own choices from shelves and racks of goods. Plastic packaging protects many items from damage. Buy a camera, for example, and you will find it inside a box and nestled in a form-fitting mold probably made of a rigid foam

Plastics, while convenient, are a huge contributor to the waste problem. While it may seem like Americans recycle a great deal of plastic, the vast majority of plastic is still tossed in the trash.

plastic. Pick up a dozen eggs from the grocery store, and they, too, are likely to be packaged in light foam plastic.

Fast food restaurants depend on plastic packaging to sell convenience along with their products—plastic containers can be thrown out after use. Supermarkets sell convenience with their packaged products, too. How about those plastic squeeze bottles that are not only shatter-proof but also allow you to dispense ketchup and mustard with ease and without much mess? Squeezable containers are made of several kinds of plastic, which gives the bottles their shape, flexibility, and strength.

GROWTH OF PLASTIC GOODS—AND WASTE

Plastics were first produced during the early 1900s. But they developed rapidly during World War II, when they were used as substitutes for scarce materials—particularly metals. The versatility, light weight, and strength of plastic materials made them ideal for a variety of military purposes and later for consumer goods. Those consumer products have increased dramatically over the years. Plastic products seem to be all around us—plastic containers, water bottles, disposable plates and utensils, phones, tablets, computer keyboards, snack containers, pens, and countless other items.

There are frozen foods packaged in plastic bags that can be boiled or microwaved right in their containers. Beverage bottles, milk jugs and containers of syrup and shampoo are made of break-resistant plastic. A variety of plastic bags are used to keep foods such as bread and produce fresh. Many other common products household items come encased in a variety of plastic materials. And in many stores purchases are placed in plastic bags for customers to carry out. The use of plastics releases at least one hundred million tons, and maybe as many as five hundred million tons, of carbon dioxide into the atmosphere each year.

"The average American throws away approximately 185 pounds of plastic per year," and recovers "only 5 percent of the plastics we produce," according to EcoWatch.com. "Plastic accounts for around 10 percent of the total waste we generate." Among that waste are thirty-five billion plastic water bottles tossed out each year.[1]

Worldwide, "the use of plastics for consumer products has become increasingly dominant, and production has steadily increased since the material was first put into wide use a half century ago. In 2012, for example, 288 million tons of plastic were manufactured globally," wrote Laura Parker for *National Geographic*. Much of that plastic ends up in the world's oceans. "Ocean plastic has turned up literally everywhere. It has been found in the deep sea and buried in Arctic ice. It has been ingested with dire consequences by some 700 species of marine wildlife."[2]

Because plastic products have such a long life, they are hazardous for many kinds of sea life. For example, sea lions, seabirds, and turtles become entangled in discarded plastic rings made to hold beverage cans and choke to death or starve because they cannot move. Or they mistake plastic bags or small pellets—waste from plastic manufacturing plants

Too often, plastic waste ends up in our oceans and endangers both the environment and the wildlife.

that have washed onto beaches—for food. When animals and birds swallow plastic materials, they may suffer internal injuries or a false feeling of fullness that makes them stop eating, thus the starve themselves.

THE SLOW DECOMPOSITION OF PLASTIC BAGS

Most plastic shopping bags are made of polyethylene, a chemical compound derived from oil. Microorganisms that biodegrade food waste do not recognize polyethylene polymers, so technically a plastic bag does not biodegrade. However, polyethylene does break down when exposed to the ultraviolet radiation from the sun. The polyethylene becomes brittle and cracks, which turns the plastic bag into microscopic synthetic granules. "Scientists aren't sure whether these granules ever decompose fully and fear that their buildup in marine and terrestrial environments–and in the stomachs of wildlife–portend a bleak future compromised by plastic particles infiltrating every step in the food chain. A plastic bag might be gone in anywhere from 10 to 100 years (estimates vary) if exposed to the sun, but its environmental legacy may last forever," reports *IndyWeek*, a weekly newspaper published in Durham, North Carolina.[3]

REDUCING USE OF PLASTICS

Burning could dramatically reduce the amount of plastic waste, but "plastic in incinerators releases toxic heavy metals and chemicals. Incinerators produce a variety of toxic discharges to the air, water, and ground that are significant sources of powerful pollutants, including dioxin and other chlorinated organic compounds that are well known for their toxic effects on human health and the environment," states Eureka! Recycling, a zero-waste organization located in the Twin Cities of Minneapolis and

Saint Paul. "Many of these toxins enter the food supply and become more concentrated as they move up through the food chain. In addition to air and water emissions, incinerators create toxic ash—or slag—which contains heavy metals, dioxins, and other pollutants. This toxic ash must be landfilled, and the pollutants present in the ash can then leach into groundwater."[4]

In some states, legislators have enacted outright bans on certain plastic products. Maine has banned the use of juice bottles made with layers of different types of plastic. In 2014, California became the first state to ban single-use plastic bags at large retail stores. The law went into effect in July 2015. The District of Columbia now has a law banning the distribution of disposable, nonrecyclable plastic bags and charges a five-cent fee for distribution of all other disposable bags. New Jersey and Puerto Rico have legislation pending that would ban single-use bags. New Jersey

A grocery store worker places items in a canvas bag. Some cities and states are starting to charge a fee for or place an outright ban on plastic bags.

TYPES OF RECYCLABLE PLASTIC

Industrialized nations produce more than twenty different types of plastic that are categorized by the types of resins used to manufacture them. The Society of Plastic Industries developed codes for types of plastics that are recyclable. The codes and numbers are shown within these triangles:

The number 1 code stands for PET or PETE, or polyethylene terephterephthalate, which is used for soft drink, water, and beer bottles, mouthwash bottles, peanut butter containers, salad dressing and vegetable oil containers, heatable food trays, and other items. PET is recycled into various products.

Code number 2 is for high density polyethylene, or HDPE, which is used for a great variety of products ranging from bleach and detergent bottles to picnic tables. It is recycled to manufacture many goods.

The letter V in Code 3 stands for vinyl or PVC, a plastic made of chlorine, carbon, and oil or gas derivatives. PVC is used to make a variety of containers that are recyclable.

Code 4 is for LDPE, or low density polyethylene, a flexible plastic with many applications. LDPE materials are recyclable.

Code 5 is PP, or polypropylene, which is a heat-resistant, flexible plastic. Products made with PP can be recycled.

Code 6 is PS, or polystyrene, which is used to produce egg cartons, disposable plates and cups, foam packing materials, and other items. Many recycling programs do not accept polystyrene.

Code 7 is for miscellaneous plastics—those that are made from a variety of resins and do not fit any of the six other categories. These plastics are recyclable.

lawmakers are also looking at a five-cent fee on disposable carryout bags, according to the National Conference of State Legislatures.

The bans on plastic bags are significant because of their link to climate change. "An estimated 12 million barrels of oil are used to manufacture the 30 million plastic bags that Americans use each year. That is equivalent to the amount of oil in our Strategic Oil Reserve. When used for bags, it is a wasteful way to deplete our oil supply and contribute to CO_2 build-up in our atmosphere," according to 1 Bag at a Time, a company that manufactures reusable fabric bags.

Cities, too, have passed anti-plastic legislation. In St. Paul and Minneapolis, ordinances decree that all food and beverage packaging must be environmentally acceptable—that is, degradable, recyclable, or returnable. Such products as plastic egg cartons and ketchup bottles are banned.

TAKE ACTION!

For a week or two, check out the codes on plastic throwaways in your household and collect them for recycling.

PROBLEMS RECYCLING PLASTIC

To date, only about 9 percent of the plastic manufactured each year is recycled. Most plastic materials that are recycled are used to make products quite different from their original form. Sixteen-ounce soft drink bottles made of PET are the most common recyclable containers. Manufacturers process PET bottles to make fibers ranging from carpet yarns to rope, fluffy fill for sleeping bags and pillows, and such products as scouring pads, fence posts, and parking space bumpers. HDPE containers—milk and water jugs, for example) are turned into flower pots, toys, pails, trash cans, speed control bumps, and a variety of synthetic lumber products, such as outdoor furniture and playground structures. Used vinyl may be refabricated to make pipes and fittings, floor tile, truck bed liners, and insect traps.

Then there are polystyrene materials the plastic foam products such as the clamshells that hold sandwiches from fast food restaurants. These foam products are often incorrectly called Styrofoam. "Technically, Styrofoam is a trademarked polystyrene product of Dow Chemical used in such applications as building insulation and craft products, not in food containers," wrote Matthew Daneman for *USA Today*.[5]

You may soon notice that your takeout food comes in a different container. Major cities across the country are starting to ban the use of polystyrene, often called Styrofoam, due to health concerns.

Benzene, a carcinogen, is used to produce polystyrene. Foods and drinks in direct contact with the foam packaging are affected by benzene. That is one of the main reasons why more than one hundred cities in the United States have banned the use of polystyrene products. Among the cities with bans are Portland, Oregon; San Francisco, California; San Jose, California; Seattle, Washington; Brookline, Massachusetts; and Washington, DC.

Corporations are also eliminating the use of foam products. McDonald's quit using clamshells for burgers in 1990, and its fourteen thousand restaurants began wrapping food in paper. McDonald's also uses paper cups rather than foam containers for beverages.

Nevertheless, throwaway plastic foam containers litter landscapes and waterways and create environmental hazards. For decades, some consumer groups and environmental organizations have been highly

TAKE ACTION!

There are numerous ways to reduce plastic use. Here are a few.

- Pack your lunch in a reusable container.
- Don't use plastic eating utensils, and ask restaurants not to pack them with your carry out.
- Carry your drinking water in a reusable container rather than separate plastic throwaways.
- Buy foods such as pasta, rice, nuts, and dried fruit from bulk bins and place in reusable containers.

critical of the increasing use of polystyrene containers. Some would like to find a way to recycle plastic foam, while others would like use of the products eliminated altogether.

DEALING WITH PLASTIC WASTE

The chemical characteristics that make plastic versatile and strong also prevent breakdown of the materials except by burning or oxidation over long periods of time. Plastics are made from synthetic resins, which are produced from natural resources such as oil and coal. Each molecule of resin is made up of long chains of hydrogen and carbon atoms, called polymers. The polymers are so tightly bound together that bacteria and fungi, which usually break down organic materials, cannot penetrate the chain. Thus, plastic materials are almost indestructible.

Producing degradable plastics is one effort to deal with the problem of plastic wastes. One type of degradable plastic photodegrades, or breaks down, when exposed to the ultraviolet rays of the sun. Through a chemical process, light-sensitive molecules, called carbonyls, are added to plastic polymers—that is, light-sensitive chemicals are mixed with the plastic resin. In sunlight, the chemicals weaken the polymers, which break down and become shorter. Eventually the plastic breaks into small fragments and decomposes.

Biochemists also combine synthetic resins with natural polymers of cornstarch or cellulose and vegetable oil to make plastic biodegradable. Bacteria feed on the natural polymers, which promote their growth, then they attack plastic polymers that might not appeal to them otherwise.

A PLASTIC-EATING BACTERIA MAY BE IN YOUR KITCHEN

Some scientific studies have shown that bacteria can degrade polyethelene if it is first exposed to light or heat. Researchers at Beihang University in China reported in December 2014 that they found chemical evidence of a bacteria that can break down plastic in one step. The Chinese researchers studied larvae of Indian mealmoths, which go by a variety of names, whose guts are filled with microbes that can digest plastic. Mealmoths are common pests found in kitchens worldwide, and their larvae consume grains, pet foods, and other mealy products. The larvae, known as waxworms, degrade polyethylene and may eventually be a possible method to biodegrade plastic.

A number of degradable plastic products are already on the market, such as biodegradable bags and disposable diapers. A growing number of communities require the use of degradable grocery and waste disposal bags. Although degradable plastics might eliminate some litter, they do not seem to be the answer to the problem of growing waste heaps in landfills. No matter what the structure of the plastic, it cannot break down in any short period of time when entombed in a landfill without sunlight and air. Second, if degradable plastics do decompose, there is the question of what happens to the shards of plastic that are left. Scientists have not yet learned precisely how the materials react when burned, buried in a landfill, or recycled with nondegradable plastics. And no one is sure about the exact amount of toxic chemicals from plastics that are released into the air, soil, and water.

Plastic companies also contend that production of degradable plastics might convince the public that plastic recycling is not needed. Recycling is

These bottle caps are made from biodegradable plastic. One is new and the other has been in seawater for sixty days.

the type of action that some plastic manufacturers favor. In fact, in 2014, Dow Chemical—along with the Flexible Packaging Association, Republic Services, the waste-to-energy plant Agilyx, Reynolds Consumer Products, and the city of Citrus Heights, California—jointly sponsored a pilot program "intended to divert non-recycled plastics from landfills and convert them into energy. From June to August 2014, approximately twenty-six thousand households in Citrus Heights received purple bags, known as Energy Bags. Participants agreed to collect plastic items not currently eligible for mechanical recycling so they could be converted into energy.

"Collected items included juice pouches, candy wrappers, plastic pet food bags, frozen food bags, laundry pouches, and plastic dinnerware," Dow explained on its website. After the Energy Bags were collected during regular trash pickups, they were sorted at a recycling facility and sent to Agilyx, which "converted the previously non-recycled plastics into high-value synthetic crude oil. The crude oil can be further refined and made into valuable products for everyday use such as gasoline, diesel fuel, jet fuel, fuel oil, lubricants, and can even be transformed back into plastic." Dow reported that "During the three-month program, there were six collection cycles resulting in:

- Nearly 8,000 purple Energy Bags collected
- Approximately 6,000 pounds of typically non-recycled items diverted from landfills
- 512 gallons of synthetic crude oil produced from the conversion."[6]

In spite of efforts to deal with various kinds of plastic waste, an ideal solution would be for biochemists and manufacturers to redesign plastic products so that all of them are nontoxic, recyclable, and do not emit greenhouse gases that contribute to climate change.

CHAPTER 7

HAZARDOUS AND TOXIC WASTES

PERHAPS YOU THROW A FLUORESCENT LIGHTBULB OR some lead-based paint in the trash, without thinking of either product as something harmful. But both are classified as hazardous wastes, as are many other items, such as cleaning fluids, degreasing solvents, pesticides, or the by-products of manufacturing processes. Other hazardous substances include asbestos—once a common construction material—batteries used electronics, waste oil, and equipment containing mercury.

The EPA classifies materials as hazardous if they are ignitable (will burn), corrosive (are acidic), reactive (could change chemically under varied conditions), or toxic (are poisonous). The EPA also makes a distinction between hazardous and toxic. Many people assume the terms are synonymous. However, hazardous waste is a general term for materials that, after lengthy exposure, could possibly damage human health and the environment. Toxic materials, if ingested or absorbed, are detrimental or fatal to living organisms.

Do not toss that used lightbulb in the trash! It is considered a hazardous waste and should be recycled accordingly.

OLD INDUSTRIAL DUMP SITES

In the past, manufacturers routinely disposed of industrial by-products and leftovers by burying the materials near factories. Industrial waste was also used as fill for wetlands or low-lying areas that were converted to construction sites or to fill in excavations left after buildings were torn down. Materials were expected to break down after being dumped on land, and it was commonly believed that soils would filter hazardous chemicals before they washed into waterways or seeped into groundwater.

Many old dump sites for industrial wastes were often called toxic time bombs. Americans became alarmed about such waste sites in 1978, when they learned about a dump near Niagara Falls, New York, called Love Canal. People living near the site developed mysterious ailments, and children were born with physical defects. Investigators soon learned that the abandoned canal had once been used as a dump site for toxic chemical wastes that had contaminated soil and drinking water, which created health hazards.

The discovery at Love Canal led to investigations of other dump sites across the United States. Within a few years, more than a thousand waste disposal areas were labeled hazardous. At the end of 1980, Congress passed the Comprehensive Environmental Response, Compensation, and Liability Act (CERCLA), which provided a superfund for cleaning up toxic waste sites. Since passage of the act, now popularly known as Superfund, Congress has allocated billions of dollars for the program, which the EPA overseas.

"Superfund Cleanup is either paid for by the parties responsible for contamination or by the Superfund Trust Fund," according to the EPA. "Under the Superfund law, EPA is able to make those companies and individuals responsible for contamination at a Superfund site perform, and pay for, the cleanup work at the site. EPA negotiates with the responsible parties to get them to pay for the plans and the work that has to be done to clean up the site. If an agreement cannot be reached, EPA issues orders to responsible parties to make them clean up the site under EPA supervision. EPA may also use Superfund Trust Fund money to pay for cleanup costs, then attempt to get the money back through legal action."[1]

As of 2014, the EPA listed more than thirteen hundred waste disposal sites that were in need of priority cleanup—in the agency's parlance they are on the National Priorities List (NPL). Most are in the northeastern and southeastern states and on the West Coast. The sites may be old landfills, burial grounds for drums of toxic wastes from chemical plants, petroleum refiners, and other industries. Some sites are located at military installations and nuclear weapons plants.

Of the Superfund sites, only a few hundred have been totally decontaminated. The process can take two to three decades to complete. In many cases, toxic wastes in a landfill are simply contained. Like other wastes, they are capped with clay. The area also is double-lined with vinyl or other synthetic material to prevent toxins from moving. Some wastes undergo chemical or biological treatment that can destroy toxic substances or prevent their movement through the ground. Or the soil with hazardous substances may be washed—drowned with water and the runoff is collected and treated to remove toxins.

The EPA also allows some hazardous waste to be burned at high temperatures in incinerators. But many environmental groups are protesting this method of disposal because incinerators emit pollutants that add to greenhouse gases.

Libby, Montana, seen from the air, was placed on the Superfund list in 2002. Pollution caused by asbestos from nearby mines killed four hundred of its residents and sickened more than a thousand. The EPA has spent many millions of dollars cleaning up the pollution and today considers the site a success story.

CLEANING UP

Communities in almost every state have been struggling for years to determine how to handle hazardous waste. One example is the Lowry Landfill, a waste site southeast of Denver, Colorado, which the city and county of Denver own. During the 1960s and 1970s, many businesses, industries, and even the US Mint dumped waste at the landfill, which contaminated soil and groundwater on the site. In 1984, the EPA placed the landfill on its National Priorities List. While the landfill accepted municipal waste for a time, it stopped taking all waste in 1990.

After an initial study of the health and environmental risks of the contamination, the EPA determined that the cleanup plan would be containment—that is, hazardous materials could not be removed because of contamination risks during transportation. According to the EPA, "A 200-acre soil cover now covers the main landfill, and an 8,800-foot long underground groundwater barrier wall of soil and clay encloses the west, east and south sides of the main landfill. Water from the north side of the site is collected for treatment. Additionally, a landfill gas collection system was installed," which extracts gas to be used as fuel to generate electricity.[2] Private businesses, municipalities, and state and federal agencies have paid for the Lowry landfill cleanup at a cost of more than $100 million.

TOXIC EMISSIONS

Although some industries are making efforts to clean up or reduce toxic wastes, manufacturing and processing plants across the nation are still sources for many toxic pollutants. In the past, no one knew what kinds of substances factories released. Members of Congress became concerned about the problem after a 1984 leak of toxic chemicals from a Union Carbide plant in Bhopal, India. The chemical emissions killed three thousand people and injured fifty thousand more.

In 1986, Congress enacted amendments to the Superfund act, which gave the EPA authority to require industries to report the types of chemicals they use or discharge into the environment. Citizens also have the right to request information about chemical hazards in their communities. In addition, cities and towns are required to develop disaster plans to deal with chemical spills or leaks.

Toxic emissions come primarily from refineries, chemical industries, and coal-fired power plants. "Coal plants are the nation's top source of carbon dioxide (CO_2) emissions, the primary cause of global warming," declared the Union of Concerned Scientists. "In 2011, utility coal plants in the United States emitted a total of 1.7 billion tons of CO_2."[3]

In 2013, the EPA says, direct industrial greenhouse gases made up about 21 percent of all US greenhouse gas emissions. This makes them the third largest contributor to the country's greenhouse gas emissions. Only the electronics and transportation sectors contribute more greenhouse gases. The agency explained:

> **Direct emissions** are produced by burning fuel for power or heat, through chemical reactions, and from leaks from industrial processes or equipment. Most direct emissions come from the consumption of fossil fuels for energy. A smaller amount, roughly a third, come from leaks from natural gas and petroleum systems, the use of fuels in production (e.g., petroleum products used to make plastics), and chemical reactions during the production of chemicals, iron and steel, and cement.

> **Indirect emissions** are produced by burning fossil fuel at a power plant to make electricity, which is then used by an industrial facility to power industrial buildings and machinery. . . . If both direct and indirect emissions associated with electricity use are included, industry's share of total US greenhouse gas emissions in 2013 was 29%, making it the largest contributor of greenhouse gases of any sector. Greenhouse gas emissions from industry have declined by almost 12% since 1990, while emissions from most other sectors have increased.[4]

In April 2015, the EPA released an updated set of 'mission factors. These are mathematical formulas used by industry to calculate the amount of air pollutants being given off by their facilities," InsideClimate News.com reported. "The new emission factors acknowledge that refinery and chemical plant flares release four times as many volatile organic compounds (VOCs) than previously thought. VOCs are dangerous chemicals that can cause cancer and other illnesses."[5]

CONTROLLING TOXIC WASTES

In efforts to get rid of toxic wastes, some communities are turning to waste haulers who specialize in hazardous waste disposal—a fast-growing and profitable business. Major haulers dump hazardous wastes in landfills they have set up under strict federal guidelines. But some firms ship waste across international borders. Shipments of hazardous materials from the United States have gone to such nations as Haiti, South Africa, Japan, Mexico, and Canada. Other industrialized nations, including Germany, Italy, Great Britain, and New Zealand, also export their toxic waste. Most of it goes to developing countries, where dumping costs are low and regulations to control pollutants barely exist.

Some receiving countries and environmental groups with international ties, such as Greenpeace, are protesting the practice, however. Caribbean and African nations have called for a complete ban on wastes from foreign sources. The United Nations Environmental Program has proposed an international treaty that would regulate and reduce the toxic waste shipments across international borders.

Within the United States, demands have increased for strict regulations to control hazardous waste disposal. The EPA has offered thousands of dollars in rewards to people who provide information leading to conviction of polluters. EPA's Criminal Enforcement Counsel is responsible for prosecuting offenders.

For a long time, Greenpeace has protested exporting hazardous waste across international borders. In this photo, members object to France sending nuclear waste to Russia.

Yet controlling toxic waste requires much more than whistle-blowing. The Federal Bureau of Investigation (FBI) has been working with the EPA since 1982 to investigate illegal transport, storage, and disposal of hazardous wastes. Some waste haulers and industries have illegally dumped toxic materials rather than dispose of them in a safe and more costly manner. Federal laws ban disposal of any chemicals that have not been treated. People who deliberately pollute for profit or through carelessness can be prosecuted.

At the state level, some legislatures have passed waste disposal laws that are more stringent than federal controls. This policy is particularly true regarding laws to combat careless disposal of medical waste. The laws were prompted by well-publicized incidents of medical debris that included bloody bandages and used syringes washing up on seacoast beaches during the summers of 1987 and 1988. Within that same period, children in Indianapolis, Indiana, found discarded blood vials in an unlocked Dumpster behind a medical clinic and playfully smashed the vials against a wall. One of the vials contained blood from a victim of AIDS. In another incident, Ohio children found medical syringes in an open Dumpster and jabbed each other with the needles as they played doctor.

Waste from hospitals and clinics does not fall under federal hazardous waste regulations. States determine guidelines for biomedical waste. In Florida, for example, there are approximately thirty-eight thousand facilities that generate such waste. These include hospitals, clinics, nursing homes, laboratories, funeral homes, dentists, veterinarians, physicians, pharmacies that provide flu shots, body piercing salons, tattoo shops, transporters, and storage and treatment facilities. The objective of the biomedical waste program is to protect healthcare workers, environmental-service staff, waste haulers, and the general public from risks associated with potentially infectious biomedical waste.

Other states have similar guidelines. Kansas, for example, mandates that medical waste must be placed in containers that are closable, constructed to contain all contents and prevent leakage of fluids, and closed prior to removal. The containers must be labeled or color-coded and must have the BIOHAZARD marking or have red bags. The facility may process the medical waste by incineration or sterilization. If there is no danger of disease or injury, the waste can then be sent to a municipal solid waste landfill.

Some states have adopted new laws or revised old regulations to toughen requirements for the treatment of medical waste. Others have set up systems to track waste from a medical facility to a disposal site and have established penalties for unsafe handling of medical waste.

States have also enacted legislation that places more rigid controls on industrial producers of hazardous materials. Massachusetts, for one, requires that industries reduce toxic emissions. The state's Department of Environmental Protection provides technical assistance for companies that are slow to cut back toxic waste, and the University of Lowell conducts research on alternatives to toxic chemical use in industry.

CLEAN UP TECHNOLOGY

"Are we cleaning up the mess or messing up the cleanup?" is the question asked in an introduction to case studies of Superfund sites. Although some studies show that cleanup activities can take decades to complete, they also show that some efforts have been fairly successful. Usually, several kinds of treatment are involved in cleanup operations, including waste disposal in mass-burners and detoxifying groundwater, which can take twenty to forty years. Some industries are handling hazardous wastes on site by injecting toxins into deep wells and storing the materials far below the aquifer, or supply of water used for drinking.

In some cases, a technology called in situ vitrification or in situ chemical reduction is employed. Long used in France, where vitrification first developed, and in other European countries and Canada, the process involves separating highly radioactive materials, called sludge, from other substances in liquid waste. The radioactive sludge is combined with clay or sand, and the mixture is heated and transformed into molten glass that is poured into steel canisters to harden for storage. Workers insert electrodes into contaminated soil, heat it, and turn it into a hard glassy material. The EPA describes the process this way:

> In situ chemical reduction, or ISCR, uses chemicals called reducing agents to help change contaminants into less toxic or less mobile forms. It is described as "in situ" because it is conducted in place, without having to excavate soil or pump groundwater above ground for cleanup. ISCR can clean up several types of contaminants dissolved in groundwater. It can also be used to clean up contaminants . . . which do not dissolve easily in groundwater and can be a source of contamination for a long time. ISCR is most often used to clean up the metal chromium and the industrial solvent[s].[6]

Scientists also have found that bacteria clean up toxic and even nuclear wastes. But how the bacteria worked was a mystery until researchers at

Michigan State University announced that they had unraveled the progression. In 2013 David Rothbard explained on CFact.org:

> As it turns out, bacteria like Geobacter have tiny, hair-like appendages known as nanowires that conduct electricity and can basically electroplate and immobilize radioactive material like uranium. The nanowires also shield the bacteria, and allow them to thrive in toxic environments. . . . [R]esearchers can use genetic engineering to produce bacteria with extra nanowires, and the microbes can generate electricity while cleaning up nasty messes.[7]

In spite of possibilities for cleaning up hazardous waste, a 2014 report from the Center for Investigative Reporting (CIR) and the Guardian US does not present an optimistic outlook. The report describes what happens in Mountain View, California, in the center of Silicon Valley, where chemical toxins from technology companies have contaminated underground water supplies. Pumps and pipes bring water to the surface and filters capture toxins, but that is only the beginning of the effort to decontaminate drinking water. As CIROnline.com reported:

> Once [toxic waste] leaves Mountain View, Calif., [it] gets shipped, treated and burned in places like Oklahoma and Arizona, discharging waste in small towns and on a Native American reservation, and in some cases creating even more harmful chemicals. . . . Along the way, waste treatment plants rack up environmental violations, records show. Byproducts created during treatment are shuttled from one plant to another. And then another. After crisscrossing

Scientists have discovered bacteria that will actually eat toxic chemicals. In this photo, researchers open a jar of sludge containing the bacteria that was taken from a polluted river. They hope to grow the bacteria in a lab and use them to clean up other rivers containing toxic pollutants.

the country, the waste even can end up right back where it started.

The CIR report depicts how toxins are treated on their route. Once the chemicals reach a site hundreds or thousands of miles away from Silicon

Valley, the toxins may be burned, which leaves toxic ash that has to be disposed of somewhere else. At the next site, ash is burned again, which reduces the toxins but does not eliminate them. "Ultimately, the trail doesn't have a single end point. Plants continually accept, treat, generate and then ship waste elsewhere to any number of different destinations. The result is a weblike network that spans the United States. On a map, it looks like fireworks bursting from treatment plants, igniting new sparks as it moves along the trail."[8]

ARE POISONS IN YOUR HOUSEHOLD?

With all the discussion about huge volumes of dangerous waste from industrial sources, it may seem senseless to raise a question about hazardous household products. But many homes can be hazardous waste sites. Household cleaners from drain openers to spot removers, paints, batteries, automotive products such as antifreeze and brake fluid, and pesticides such as insect and rodent killers are among the many products that can endanger human health and the environment.

Many consumers toss leftover chemical products into the trash along with yard and food wastes. Although hazardous household throwaways make up only a small portion of the waste stream in most communities, the material adds to the already complex problems with waste disposal at landfills.

The words from the opening paragraph of a Greenpeace flyer, "Stepping Lightly on the Earth: Everyone's Guide to Toxics in the Home," put it this way:

> Most of us like to think that the widespread contamination of our groundwater, soil and air is entirely due to the

irresponsibility of large industry. We refuse to accept the notion that in our own everyday lives we are contributing to the slow poisoning of the planet. But commonly used

We can do our part to eliminate toxic chemicals in our homes by using environmentally friendly cleaning products, such as baking soda, lemon, and vinegar.

> substances such as paint thinners, household pesticides, cleaners and solvents, and some aerosols produce hazardous waste. Our responsibility for them does not end at our curbside . . . toxic waste comes back to haunt us.[9]

The flyer, published in 1987 and still relevant today, explains how to replace chemical household cleaners with inexpensive and safe products that most people have readily available. Baking soda is a safe all-purpose cleaner and deodorizer. Other environmentally safe cleaning substances include vinegar, washing soda, lemon, lemon oil for polishing, ammonia when used with care, and borax.

With increasing awareness of pollution problems, communities across the United States have been setting up programs to collect household poisons. These may be annual events or part of ongoing recycling and waste management efforts. Some programs provide information on how to treat hazardous household wastes safely at home, suggest ways that householders can reuse or recycle goods, or, better yet, reduce their use of toxic products.

CHAPTER 8

NUCLEAR POWER AND WASTE

NUCLEAR POWER PLANTS DO NOT EMIT GREENHOUSE gases, so many Americans say that nuclear power is the cleanest source of energy. It reduces dependence on fossil fuels, which contribute to climate change. The US Energy Information Administration (EIA) reported that in 2015, there were sixty-one nuclear power plants with ninety-nine nuclear reactors in thirty states, thirty-five of which have two or more reactors.[1] These reactors produce thermal energy for electrical power.

But there is a downside. Nuclear plants also produce radioactive waste. "Currently, nuclear waste created in the US is stored underwater in spent fuel pools near nuclear power plants," according to nuclear engineers. They add that while underground storage is a suitable way to store nuclear waste, we will soon need to build more sites to accommodate the large amount of waste that has built up.[2]

The benefits and hazards of nuclear power have been debated for some time now. Some environmentalists see it as the cleanest form of power available, while others worry about the effects of radioactive waste.

In March 2015, the Union of Concerned Scientists (UCS) published a report titled *The NRC and Nuclear Power Plant Safety in 2014*. NRC stands for Nuclear Regulatory Commission, which is responsible for regulating the safety of nuclear power plants. The report emphasizes that the NRC "often claims to be the gold standard for nuclear power plant safety regulation and oversight. Ample evidence suggests much validity to these claims. One cannot count the number of nuclear disasters averted by the NRC's effective regulatory performance."

However, UCS found that the gold standard was tarnished when regulators improperly withheld information about safety problems, such as a flooding hazard at the Oconee Nuclear Station in Seneca, South Carolina in 2010. A reporter was able to obtain records of the flood in 2013 through the Freedom of Information Act. "The NRC could have, and should have, openly communicated about the situation at Oconee the same way the agency publicly communicated about similar flooding problems," the scientists' report stated.

The report also explains how the NRC tried to silence two engineers who voiced concerns over safety. The report concluded that "one can generally count on the NRC to be an effective regulator. But if the NRC truly is the gold standard, it must restore the luster and prevent the tarnish from recurring."[3]

DEBATES OVER NUCLEAR FACILITIES

Deliberations and discussions about nuclear power, weapons, and what to do with radioactive waste have been going on for decades. Some people scoff at the potential dangers of radiation. Many workers at nuclear facilities are more concerned about maintaining their jobs than about possible health effects from radiation exposure. In areas where jobs are scarce, some people say they would welcome a nuclear waste dump or other nuclear facility that would bring employment opportunities with it.

Part of the nuclear energy controversy revolves around the growing need for electricity and the fact that coal-fired power plants generate pollutants that are partially responsible for such global problems as the greenhouse effect and acid rain. Some air pollutants can be more long-lasting than radioactive materials.

On the other hand, many people fear nuclear energy and the wastes that nuclear plants generate because they believe they will be exposed to high levels of radiation from accidental leaks. Critics cite the 1979 accident at the Three Mile Island reactor in the United States and the 1986 explosion at the Chernobyl plant in the Soviet Union.

At Three Mile Island in Pennsylvania, a faulty valve prevented cooling water from circulating in the reactor, which overheated the core and melted more than half of it. As a result, radioactive emissions spewed into the air. But studies later showed that the radiation dose averaged ten millirems—about the same amount as a typical dental X-ray emits—for people within ten miles of the reactor and up to one hundred millirems for plant workers.

In the United States, radiation effects are measured in millirem units, or thousandths of a rem. In other words, one thousand millirem equals one rem. Some experts claim that there is no evidence of increased cancer rates or other health problems due to the radiation at Three Mile Island, while others argue that cancers generally do not develop for fifteen to twenty years after exposure, and they expect cancer rates in the region to rise.

The world's worst nuclear power plant accident occurred in the Soviet Ukraine, when an explosion and fire destroyed the Chernobyl plant.

Highly radioactive clouds spread over Scandinavia, England, and parts of Europe, eventually leaving thirty-one dead and thousands more facing possible health problems because of high doses of radiation.

Proponents of nuclear power, however, believe that it is one solution to energy production that does not contribute to climate change. Those who favor nuclear energy also point out that several hundred nuclear power plants worldwide safely generate electricity. Many industrialized nations are increasing their use of nuclear power without serious mishaps, proponents emphasize.

Anyone without expertise in this complex issue of nuclear power can have a difficult time sorting out the benefits and hazards. At the same time,

An abandoned playground near Three Mile Island. The 1979 meltdown there was the worst nuclear power plant disaster to occur on American soil. The incident resulted in stricter regulation for nuclear power plants across the country.

the nuclear waste controversy seems to raise more and more questions with few of them fully answered. Materials on nuclear energy and waste are available from several federal departments, including the Department of Energy, the Department of Transportation, the Nuclear Regulatory Commission, and the Environmental Protection Agency. Environmental groups also publish materials on the subject. Some selected references are listed toward the end of this book.

CATEGORIZING NUCLEAR WASTE

Whenever radioactive materials are used, they produce waste. Nuclear waste comes from defense-related activities—weapons plants and nuclear-powered ships—and from private industry, including medical facilities, laboratories, and nuclear power plants. Along with nuclear power plants, reactors also produce valuable radioisotopes used in such activities as laboratory research, making clock dials luminous, and detecting tumors or other physical abnormalities in people. Another source of nuclear waste is uranium mining. When uranium ore is processed at a mill, the tailings, or leftovers, contain small amounts of radioactive elements that occur naturally.

In the United States, the federal government uses six different categories to define nuclear waste. But in broad terms, wastes can be classified as low-level or high-level depending on how much radioactivity is emitted. Radioactivity begins to take place as soon as an atom splits, which releases energy, or radiation, in the form of particles, or rays. As the number of atoms decreases, so does the rate of radioactive emission, which is said to decay. The rate of decay is measured by half-life, or the time it takes for half the atoms of a radioactive substance to disintegrate to another nuclear form. Half-lives vary from fractions of a second to billions of years.

What effect does radiation have on people? That depends on the amount of radiation and the length of time a person is exposed. The Jefferson Lab, which is one of seventeen national laboratories funded by the US Department of Energy, explains it this way:

> If you receive a chest x-ray, the amount of exposure—or *dose*—would be approximately 10 mrem (0.010 rem). This same amount of dose, or biological harm, could be received from making two or three coast to coast airline flights—each round trip involves about 5 mrem (from elevated cosmic radiation levels in the upper atmosphere). The important point is, the source of the exposure is relatively unimportant.[4]

Scientists worldwide have debated whether or not low-level radiation over long periods of time creates health risks. As radiation doses increase, the risks to human health appear to increase, as well. Large doses of radiation have been linked to cancer and birth defects. Intense radiation kills large numbers of cells and may cause internal bleeding and the failure of vital organs. Exposure to large doses all at once is lethal.

The total volume of nuclear waste in the United States is small compared to that of solid waste—garbage and trash—but some high-level radioactive waste can be extremely dangerous. The nuclear fuel cycle generates most of the highly radioactive material. That cycle begins with mining uranium ore, which is converted to gas and then enriched, or processed, so it contains more U-235 atoms—the uranium isotopes that can be split apart easily. Then the gas is turned into a powdered uranium dioxide and formed into small pellets that are placed inside twelve-foot-long thin tubes called fuel rods. About two hundred rods are bundled to form a fuel assembly.

Fuel assemblies make up the core of a nuclear reactor and are surrounded by control rods that absorb neutrons and determine the speed of the fission reaction. When the control rods are in place, fission slows down, but when the rods are pulled out, the speed of the chain reaction increases. Steel and concrete around the core prevent radiation from escaping.

During the fission process, hundreds of different types of by-products are created. These fission products, as they are called, are solids or gases. In addition, when uranium atoms absorb neutrons but do not fission, they become elements known as transuranics. Plutonium is one of them. Radioactive fission products and transuranics accumulate but are locked inside the fuel rods.

As fuel assemblies absorb more and more neutrons, fission slows down. Thus every three or four years, the assemblies must be replaced. At federal facilities, spent fuel from nuclear reactors is recycled. That is, the assemblies go to processing plants on the site, and uranium and plutonium are recovered for use in nuclear weapons.

Since some of the by-products in the spent fuel rods remain radioactive for many thousands to millions of years, the assemblies are immediately stored underwater in pools—rather like swimming pools—near the reactors. Water circulates around the assemblies, cools the spent fuel, and acts as a radiation shield. Although some spent fuel rods have been in storage pools since the 1960s, the cooling ponds were meant to serve only as temporary storage facilities until the radioactive material could be treated and placed in a permanent waste disposal site. But developing a place to store high-level nuclear waste is costly and controversial.

Like landfills, nuclear storage pools are filling up. States where commercial nuclear reactors are located are concerned about what effects these pools may be having on the environment. High-level waste from commercial reactors is regulated by the federal government, but over the years, federal facilities have had a poor track record regarding management of their own nuclear wastes—materials generated from reactors and weapons plants.

A nuclear storage pool in France, where spent nuclear fuel tanks are placed under water to lower their temperature. Experts are worried that we cannot keep up with the need for places to store nuclear waste.

WHAT TO DO WITH LOW-LEVEL WASTE?

All the problems at weapons plants and questions about what to do with highly radioactive nuclear waste have created concerns about the disposal of low-level radioactive waste. Low-level nuclear waste includes such things as discarded gloves and clothing used by nuclear plant workers, some resins from power plants, and radioactive materials from hospitals and laboratories. It is the kind of waste that people want to keep out of their backyard, although experts claim the radioactivity of the waste is generally short-lived.

Because of limited facilities for nuclear waste, federal law now mandates that individual states or a compact, or group, of states take responsibility for disposing of low-level nuclear wastes generated within their boundaries. It is an issue that has aroused many not-in-my-backyard (NIMBY) protests in many communities across the nation.

People who live near proposed waste sites fear that their soil and water will be contaminated. However, some environmental and civic groups are taking part in the process of determining where nuclear waste facilities will be located and how they will be designed.

One site that is operating is the Waste Isolation Pilot Plant located in southeast New Mexico about twenty-six miles from Carlsbad. It is an underground repository carved out of a two-thousand-foot-thick salt bed formed 250 million years ago, where transuranic (TRU) waste is deposited in rooms mined from the salt. The waste consists of clothing, tools, rags, residues, debris, soil, and other items contaminated with small amounts of plutonium and other human-made radioactive elements. "TRU waste is long-lived and has to be isolated to protect public health and the environment. Deep geologic disposal in salt beds was chosen because the salt is free of flowing water, easily mined, impermeable and geologically stable. Salt rock also naturally seals fractures and closes openings," the DOE explained.[5]

NUCLEAR WEAPONS

For many years, nuclear weapons plants were operated in secret with little oversight from Congress or federal regulatory agencies. The facilities were closed to public scrutiny because of what some have called an overzealous concern about national security. When the Atomic Energy Commission was dissolved in 1974, several federal agencies took over responsibilities for nuclear weapons protection and management of nuclear waste. In 1977, the US Department of Energy (DOE) was formed, and one of its main assignments was nuclear research and development, which includes plans for nuclear waste disposal.

In the past, it was common practice to dump some radioactive wastes from the manufacture of weapons directly into burial pits or leaky ponds. According to the conventional wisdom decades ago, "dilution was the solution to pollution." In other words, the experts theorized that large volumes of air, soil, and water would dilute contaminants so they would not be hazardous to public health. However, laboratory tests of spring water near the Hanford Reservation in Washington, a weapons plant that was permanently closed in 1987, showed levels of radioactive materials one thousand times higher than federal standards now allow for drinking water.

The DOE oversees the nuclear weapons facilities. Since 1987, some federal government studies and private investigations, such as the UCS study, have shown that the DOE has been lax in its oversight responsibilities. The studies document mechanical failures and lack of safety precautions at weapons plants plus contamination of the environment from nuclear waste disposal.

TAKE ACTION!

Check the Internet to find out where nuclear plants are located near your community and send messages to members of Congress to request information about their safety.

WASTE FROM NUCLEAR WEAPONS

The problem of waste from nuclear weapons facilities has been festering since the United States began to build atomic bombs in the 1940s. At that time, the federal Atomic Energy Commission (AEC) was set up to oversee production of an atomic, or nuclear, bomb that would help end World War II. An atomic bomb explodes because of fission—unstable uranium atoms called isotopes split into parts. As the isotopes split, they release neutrons, tiny atomic particles, which hit other uranium atoms. This fissions the atoms in a continual chain reaction that creates more and more heat and eventually causes an explosion.

During the 1950s, the United States and Great Britain developed hydrogen bombs, and they were declared to be one thousand times more powerful than atomic bombs. When a hydrogen bomb explodes, atoms split and then join together in a process called fusion that generates vast amounts of energy. The hydrogen bomb was not used in war, but the United States continued to build nuclear weapons. It was a long-standing defense policy of the United States to build enough weapons so other nations would be afraid to attack—maintaining a so-called balance of terror.

Nuclear weapons plants were built in such states as Washington, Colorado, Ohio, Tennessee, and South Carolina. For more than forty years, atomic reactors at the US Hanford Reservation in Washington state burned uranium to produce plutonium, which also fissions and is used to make nuclear weapons. Although plutonium occurs in small amounts in nature, the metal is primarily the by-product of carefully controlled fission in nuclear reactors. In 1950, reactors at the Savannah River Plant in South Carolina began producing not only plutonium but also another by-product, tritium, which is a form of hydrogen used in the manufacture of warheads for nuclear missiles.

The United States stopped producing nuclear weapons decades ago, but the nation still has thousands of nuclear warheads.

Disposing of nuclear weapons and handling nuclear waste properly has become an issue for politicians, as well as scientists and environmentalists. Here, Barack Obama, a senator at the time, meets with former employees of nuclear weapons plants to discuss compensation for illnesses related to their exposure to radioactive materials.

CLEANUP ACTIVITIES

The DOE's Office of Environmental Management (EM) is responsible for dismantling and cleaning up nuclear weapons facilities and contracting with private companies to do the work. The EM "has been charged with the responsibility of cleaning up 107 sites across the country whose area is equal to the combined area of Rhode Island and Delaware. EM has made substantial progress in nearly every area of nuclear waste cleanup and as of September 2012, completed cleanup at 90 of these sites," according to the DOE.[6]

> Cleanup activities include treating and permanently disposing of millions of gallons of radioactive and chemical waste stored in large underground tanks; disposing of spent nuclear fuel; removing contaminated soil; treating contaminated groundwater; packaging and shipping solid wastes infused with synthetic radioactive elements like plutonium and americium for permanent disposal to a deep geologic repository; and eliminating excess facilities, which may include decontaminating, decommissioning, deactivating, and demolishing obsolete structures or a combination of these activities.[7]

At the closed Hanford Reservation in southeastern Washington, cleanup has been underway for decades. The Hanford site consists of 586 square miles. According to Valarie Brown's article in *Scientific American*:

> The most toxic and voluminous nuclear waste in the U.S.—208 million liters [56 million gallons]—sits in decaying underground tanks at the Hanford Site. It accumulated

> there from the middle of World War II . . . to 1987, when the last reactor shut down. The federal government's current attempt at a permanent solution for safely storing that waste . . . has hit a major snag in the form of potential chain reactions, hydrogen explosions and leaks from metal corrosion.

The cost for cleaning up the site is now estimated at $13.4 billion and will not begin until 2022. The future of the Hanford Site is still in question, "The real question, many Hanford watchers say, is whether the country wants to pay for doing it right."[8]

Where will high-level nuclear waste—not only from Hanford but also from other sites—eventually be stored? That is a question many local, state, and federal government officials would like answered. In 1982, Congress passed the Nuclear Waste Policy Act, which mandates a detailed procedure to be completed for disposal of high-level nuclear waste in rock formations deep underground. Nuclear scientists and geologists around the world generally agree that isolating the material for thousands of years will protect the environment and people from radiation hazards.

The experts' conclusions are based not only on laboratory analyses and experiments but also on a discovery of a natural nuclear reactor that existed 1.8 billion years ago in Africa. Deep underground, a fission chain reaction took place in a vein of uranium ore saturated with water. This natural reactor operated for thousands of years and produced the same kind of radioactive waste produced by nuclear power plants built in this century. Studies of the area have shown that the radioactive materials, including plutonium, remained stable and decayed slowly into nonradioactive elements. Other countries that operate nuclear power systems—Argentina, Canada, France, Italy, Japan, Sweden, and Germany, among them—also plan to dispose of high-level waste in deep underground formations.

Since 1987, a storage facility has been planned for Yucca Mountain, Nevada, one hundred miles northwest of Las Vegas in the Mojave Desert. The Yucca Mountain site would be the repository for canisters of high-level radioactive materials. However, there have been many delays, as geologists, engineers, environmentalists, and politicians debate the safety of the site.

In 2012, President Obama's administration appointed an independent commission, the Nuclear Regulatory Commission (NRC), to analyze the nation's nuclear waste policies. Three years later, in 2015, the NRC declared that building "a nuclear waste repository at Yucca Mountain, Nevada, is technically sound," and there is little risk of radiation over millions of years.[9]

Nevertheless, there are still political debates about the site. Some of Nevada's leaders do not want the site in their backyard even though a federal law has designated Yucca Mountain as a permanent repository for nuclear waste. In other areas of the nation, opponents argue that no new nuclear power plants should be built until there is a federal repository for waste.

Proponents continue to advocate for building and completing the repository, but that is not expected to happen soon. The DOE estimates it will be 2048 before the site could open. In the meantime, nuclear waste continues to accumulate alongside nuclear power plants. Obviously, some action has to be taken but what, when, and how? No one knows when there will be answers that satisfy politicians, environmentalists, industrialists, and most American citizens.

CHAPTER 9

HELP SAVE OUR PLANET

AS CONSUMERS, MANUFACTURERS, RETAIL BUSINESSES, politicians, government regulators, and scientists struggle with ways to reduce waste, there is a growing public recognition that waste disposal represents only one part of interrelated environmental problems. Contaminate the soil and water, and the result may be a poisoned food chain that eventually poses human health hazards. Foul the air near an industry, and greenhouse gas pollutants can spread far and wide.

People also are recognizing that actions in one part of the world can create global effects. As The Blue Planet Prize Laureats, a group of worldwide experts and leaders put it: "In the face of an absolutely unprecedented emergency, society has no choice but to take dramatic action to avert a collapse of civilization. Either we will change our ways and build an entirely new kind of global society, or they will be changed for us."[1]

The Intergovernmental Panel on Climate Change (IPCC) also warned, "Human interference with the climate system is occurring and climate

Environmental activists in New York demand changes in the government's policy on climate change.

change poses risks for human and natural systems."[2] And US Secretary of State John F. Kerry noted in a 2014 report on climate change, "It is time for all of us to do what the science tells us we must, to do what our faiths require of us, and to do what our fragile planet demands of us: It's time to take strong action to combat a truly life-and-death challenge."[3]

OTHER VOICES HEARD

Religious leaders were invited to weigh in on climate change at a United Nations summit on climate change in December 2015. Seven rabbis joined together to pen and release a petition in May 2015 titled "A Rabbinic Letter on the Climate Crisis." The rabbis called for vigorous action to prevent worsening climate disruption and to seek eco-social justice. More than 340 rabbis had signed the document as of mid-June 2015. "The signers include Reform, Conservative, Reconstructionist, and a few Orthodox rabbis from across the United States, and some from Canada," according to David O'Reilly of Philly.com.[4]

The Rabbinic Letter declared in part:

> In Leviticus 26, the Torah warns us that if we refuse to let the Earth rest, it will "rest" anyway, despite us and upon us—through drought and famine and exile that turn an entire people into refugees.
>
> This ancient warning heard by one indigenous people in one slender land has now become a crisis of our planet as a whole and of the entire human species. Human behavior that overworks the Earth—especially the overburning of fossil fuels—crests in a systemic planetary response that endangers human communities and many other life-forms as well....
>
> We believe that there is both danger and hope in American society today, a danger and a hope that the American Jewish community, in concert with our sisters and brothers in other communities of Spirit, must address. The danger is that America is the largest contributor to the scorching of our planet. The hope is that over and over in our history, when our country faced the need for profound change, it has been our communities of moral commitment, religious covenant, and spiritual search that have arisen to meet the need.[5]

On June 18, 2015, Pope Francis delivered an encyclical, or teaching document, directed to the more than one million Roman Catholics and also all people worldwide. His 184-page letter addresses the Care of Our Common Home and the issue of climate change. He wrote:

> The urgent challenge to protect our common home includes a concern to bring the whole human family together to seek a sustainable and integral development, for we know that things can change. . . .
>
> I urgently appeal, then, for a new dialogue about how we are shaping the future of our planet. We need a conversation which includes everyone, since the environmental challenge we are undergoing, and its human roots, concern and affect us all. The worldwide ecological movement has already made considerable progress and led to the establishment of numerous organizations committed to raising awareness of these challenges. Regrettably, many efforts to seek concrete solutions to the environmental crisis have proved ineffective, not only because of powerful opposition but also because of a more general lack of interest. Obstructionist attitudes, even on the part of believers, can range from denial of the problem to indifference, nonchalant resignation or blind confidence in technical solutions. We require a new and universal solidarity.[6]

He goes on to name important contributing factors for climate change and point to the "model of development based on the intensive use of fossil fuels, which is at the heart of the worldwide energy system. Another determining factor has been an increase in changed uses of the soil, principally deforestation for agricultural purposes."

The Pope and heads of other religions have called for world leaders to take action when it comes to the environment. They are in agreement that the way we have been treating the earth has put us on a dangerous path.

Protestant pastors, as well as rabbis, have embraced the Pope's encyclical, although the pontiff's letter has raised the ire of political opponents, such as Jeb Bush, former governor of Florida and a 2016 presidential candidate. In a political speech, Bush, who is a devout Catholic, said his religious leader "ought to be [talking] about making us better as people and less about things that end up getting into the political realm."[7] And former Pennsylvania Senator Rick Santorum said the Pope should "leave science to the scientists." Other critics were vocal before the Pope's letter was published. "In April [2015], the Heartland Institute, a conservative group skeptical of climate change, mounted a campaign to convince Pope Francis that global warming "is not a crisis."[8] Nevertheless, many people around the world hope or expect the words of Pope Francis, as well as other leaders and scientists, to be repeated and to prompt varied actions to alleviate climate change.

REDUCING SUPER-POLLUTANTS

Hydrofluorocarbons, or HFCs—known super-pollutants—are factory-made gases used primarily in air conditioning and refrigeration and are among the fastest growing greenhouse gases in the world. Unless fast action is taken, the emissions of HFCs in the United States are expected to nearly triple by 2030. To reduce emissions of HFCs, in 2014, President Obama directed his administration to purchase cleaner alternatives to HFCs whenever feasible and transition over time to equipment that uses safer and more sustainable alternatives. Internationally, the Administration has been working with foreign governments and other stakeholders to reduce the production and consumption of HFCs globally.[9]

WHAT CAN YOU DO?

Taking strong action seems to be easier said than done. But one way you can start is by becoming an activist for a cause such as reducing landfill waste. Fifteen-year-old Milo Cress of Colorado began a Be Straw Free campaign when he was only nine years old. He had learned that plastic straws do not disintegrate easily in a landfill. According to his campaign, five hundred million disposable straws are used in the United States each day, "enough disposable straws to fill over 46,400 large school buses per year."

Milo is not against using straws, but he believes that restaurant owners should ask people if they want a straw. Given a choice, many customers simply opt not to use a drinking straw. As Milo explained, being straw-free "is a small step for each restaurant but a huge step for the planet."[10]

Taking action to reduce greenhouse gases is a task that fourteen-year-old Xiuhtezcatl (pronounced Shoe-Tez-Caht) Martinez of Boulder, Colorado, has taken on. He grew up the Aztec way and learned from his father that "throwing a water bottle in a river will impact your community, those downstream, and eventually have a global impact. He is fighting for people to think twice about how they interact with the world," wrote Vanessa Black in EcoWatch.com. Xiuhtezcatl "is the youth director of Earth Guardians, a non-profit environmental organization that is committed to protecting the water, air, earth and atmosphere. To reach young people, Xiuhtezcatl and his younger brother Itzcuauhtli started an eco-hip-hop duo in the namesake of their non-profit, 'Earth Guardians.'"[11]

Itzcuauhtli was thirteen years old in 2015 and spent the year holding events to demonstrate that youth have power. He urged people to sign a pledge and commit to be climate leaders. One of Itzcuauhtli's actions was "a 45-day silent strike for climate action" and collecting "more than one million signatures from youth around the world to deliver to United Nations leaders . . . for the climate talks. Upon ending his silent strike, more than one and a half million engaged in his message and over 5,000 people pledged to go silent for a day in support of climate action," according to the Earth Guardians' website.[12]

HOW FOOD WASTE AFFECTS US AND THE PLANET

The Natural Resources Defense Council (NRDC), an international environmental organization, noted in a 2012 report that "40 percent of food in the United States . . . goes uneaten. That is more than 20 pounds of food per person every month. Not only does this mean that Americans are throwing out the equivalent of $165 billion each year, but also 25 percent of all freshwater and huge amounts of unnecessary chemicals, energy, and land. Moreover, almost all of that uneaten food ends up rotting in landfills where organic matter accounts for 16 percent of US methane emissions."[13] The report goes on to blame the availability of cheap food for the lack of value we place on what we buy. Many Americans do not give a second thought to throwing away food, which ultimately affects our environment, as well as the economy.[14]

Consider this: When you throw away leftovers from a fast food restaurant or school cafeteria lunch, do you have the planet and climate change on your mind? At home do you give much thought to reducing food waste? Like the NRDC noted, for many of us wasted food is not on our radar. Yet we can make a difference and help the planet by following some of these suggestions offered by a variety of online sources.

- Use a bucket or other kitchen container to hold only food scraps or leftovers for several days to raise awareness of food waste in your own household.
- Check your refrigerator to determine whether there are forgotten food items molding or rotting away on the back of a shelf.
- If you help with grocery shopping, be aware that sale items may be marked at, say, ten for ten dollars. This is not a bargain if you can't use ten. Buy only what you need at a dollar apiece, which will prevent waste and save money.
- Rather than throw away bread that is several days old, freeze it for later use.

EFFECTIVE ACTIVISTS

Characteristics that make an effective activist include enthusiasm and energy, commitment, reliability, and respect for others' views. Activists also are most effective if they are flexible, open-minded, and ready to learn something new. Other helpful attributes include the ability to maintain self-control and avoid personal attacks on those who have views that differ from yours. Sometimes being an activist means doing routine tasks, such as writing letters or sending emails to politicians, government officials, and company executives to ask them to support your cause. It is easy to get discouraged when you don't see results immediately, but keep going and look at obstacles or setbacks as challenges to overcome.

- Join an organization or food pantry that collects food for people who are among the forty-nine million Americans who cannot afford to buy what they need for survival.
- Take part in local food drives for the homeless and hungry.
- At a restaurant, ask about portion sizes, and order only what you can finish. If you do have leftovers, take them home and keep them for your next meal.

TAKE ACTION!

Develop a plan with family members to reduce daily electricity use. Ask each member of your household to be responsible for a specific action that saves on electric power, such as turning off a computer or video game at night rather than leaving the devices on. Ask your parents or guardians to keep track of electric bills to determine whether changes occur over a period of several months.

ACTIVIST IDEAS

Along with Earth Guardians, other organizations have websites urging people—young and old—to do their part to save the planet. Arbor Day Foundation, for example, helps people buy, plant, and nurture trees that conserve energy and remove pollutants from the air. The Earth Day Network explains on its website how you can take action, such as reducing your energy production, stopping use of disposable plastic, ending junk mail, and recycling electronic devices. For more activist ideas, check out the site at www.earthday.org/takeaction/campaigns.html.

You can find "50 Ways to Help the Planet" at www.50waystohelp.com. One suggestion is to buy locally grown food, which not only supports your local economy but also reduces the greenhouse gases created when products are trucked or flown in. Another idea is to go vegetarian for one day each week. "One less meat-based meal a week helps the planet and your diet. For example: It requires 2,500 gallons of water to produce one pound of beef. You will also save some trees. For each hamburger that originated from animals raised on rainforest land, approximately 55 square feet of forest have been destroyed."[15]

Earth Island Institute sponsors Youth Empowered Action (YEA) camps in three states: Oregon, California, and New York. Young people ages twelve to seventeen spend a week in the summer to learn how to make a difference in causes they care about, such as climate change, gay rights, and fighting homelessness. On the YEA website (yeacamp.org), campers

There are many ways, big and small, that you can get involved and help the environment. From starting a compost bin in your backyard to organizing an Earth Day rally, you have the power to change the future.

share their experiences. "This camp has changed my life. It has opened my eyes to the world and inspired me to go out and make a change," sixteen-year-old Katie from California wrote. "It has given me the tools and skills I need to be effective and introduced me to people who are going to change the world for the better. It has given me hope that even though it's difficult, we can make a difference."

Another sixteen-year-old, Lamanh, said, "YEA Camp was truly one of the best things that's ever happened in my life, not only as an activist, but also as a person of character and civic duty. The experience and lessons that I learned at YEA Camp are something that I'll take with me wherever I go and plan to do. I've learned such an incredible amount."[16]

Finally, it comes down to the basic recognition that the more we consume—whether is food, energy, plastics, or other materials—the more waste we generate. We also use up more natural resources and create more pollution problems for our particular space on Earth and for the planet as a whole. We do not occupy this alone. We share it with many other humans and living creatures. If we foul our own nest, do we have a right to let our waste spill over into someone else's backyard or another creature's habitat? Each of us can make a difference if we reduce consumption and don't forget the other two words in the familiar green triangle: reuse and recycle. No one wants to be buried or destroyed by too much garbage. We need to save the earth, not just for us but for all who will follow us.

APPENDIX

EXCERPT FROM ENCYCLICAL LETTER LAUDATO SI' OF the Holy Father Francis on Care for Our Common Home:

Some forms of pollution are part of people's daily experience. Exposure to atmospheric pollutants produces a broad spectrum of health hazards, especially for the poor, and causes millions of premature deaths. People take sick, for example, from breathing high levels of smoke from fuels used in cooking or heating. There is also pollution that affects everyone, caused by transport, industrial fumes, substances which contribute to the acidification of soil and water, fertilizers, insecticides, fungicides, herbicides and agrotoxins in general. Technology, which, linked to business interests, is presented as the only way of solving these problems, in fact proves incapable of seeing the mysterious network of relations between things and so sometimes solves one problem only to create others.

Account must also be taken of the pollution produced by residue, including dangerous waste present in different areas. Each year hundreds of millions of tons of waste are generated, much of it non-biodegradable, highly toxic and radioactive, from homes and businesses, from construction and demolition sites, from clinical, electronic and industrial sources. The earth, our home, is beginning to look more and more like an immense pile of filth. In many parts of the planet, the elderly lament that once beautiful landscapes are now covered with rubbish. Industrial waste and chemical products utilized in cities and agricultural areas can lead to bioaccumulation in the organisms of the local population, even when levels of toxins in those places are low. Frequently no measures are taken until after people's health has been irreversibly affected.

These problems are closely linked to a throwaway culture which affects the excluded just as it quickly reduces things to rubbish. To cite one example, most of the paper we produce is thrown away and not recycled. It is hard for us to accept that the way natural ecosystems work is exemplary: plants synthesize nutrients which feed herbivores; these in turn become food for carnivores, which produce significant quantities of organic waste which give rise to new generations of plants. But our industrial system, at the end of its cycle of production and consumption, has not developed the capacity to absorb and reuse waste and by-products. We have not yet managed to adopt a circular model of production capable of preserving resources for present and future generations, while limiting as much as possible the use of non-renewable resources, moderating their consumption, maximizing their efficient use, reusing and recycling them. A serious consideration of this issue would be one way of counteracting the throwaway culture which affects the entire planet, but it must be said that only limited progress has been made in this regard.

To read the letter in its entirety, go to:
http://i2.cdn.turner.com/cnn/2015/images/06/18/papa-francesco_20150524_enciclica-laudato-si_en.pdf

Secretary of State John Kerry's cover letter to the *United States Climate Action Report 2014*:

Climate change is one of the most urgent and profoundly complex challenges we face. That's why, everywhere I travel as Secretary of State—in every meeting, here at home and across the more than 280,000 miles I've traveled since I raised my hand and took the oath to serve in this office—I have made this issue a top priority.

Today, all the scientific evidence is telling us that we cannot afford to delay the reckoning with climate change. With each passing day, the case grows more compelling and the costs of inaction grow beyond anything that anyone with conscience or common sense should be willing to contemplate.

The IPCC's Fifth Assessment Report is another wakeup call. It marshals unassailable evidence of the perils of inaction: Summertime Arctic sea ice volume has shrunk by 70 percent since 1979, 12 of the hottest 13 years on record have occurred since 2000, and the oceans are 30 percent more acidic than they were a century ago. Bottom Line: Climate change is real, it's happening now, and human beings are the cause.

In the face of these risks and these warnings, it is time for all of us to do what the science tells us we must, to do what our faiths require of us, and to do what our fragile planet demands of us: It's time to take strong action to combat a truly life-and-death challenge.

Today, people all over the world are demanding action on climate change, and those of us in positions of authority globally have a responsibility to lead the way toward progress. The United States is committed to doing its part.

That's why I am pleased to present this 2014 Climate Action Report to the United Nations Framework Convention on Climate Change (UNFCCC). This report contains our national communication—a quadrennial report detailing actions the United States is taking at home and internationally to mitigate, adapt to, and assist others in addressing climate change as part of our commitments under the UNFCCC.

The report builds on the most authoritative assessments of climate change. It outlines U.S. efforts to promote the research, development, and deployment of technologies to reduce greenhouse gas emissions. It highlights our substantial and growing efforts to support developing countries in the global response to climate change. It also details the financial assistance education programs, and policies and measures we've implemented both to reduce greenhouse gases and to adapt to the effects of climate change.

I am especially pleased that the 2014 Climate Action Report contains the United States' first-ever Biennial Report, which outlines our plan to reduce greenhouse gas emissions trends even further through 2020. The agreement within the UNFCCC to submit biennial reports represents one of the most significant outcomes from recent negotiations. It is a critical means of ensuring that the parties are implementing the pledges they made under the Cancun decisions. The U.S. Biennial Report shows that we are working toward meeting our Cancun commitments by taking action to reduce emissions across our energy economy, as well as in the land sector.

The path to progress has been long. But I'm proud to say that we are closer than we've ever been to a breakthrough.

Under President Obama's leadership, we have doubled wind and solar electricity generation; adopted the toughest fuel economy standards for passenger vehicles in U.S. history; advanced environmental standards to expedite the transition to cleaner and more efficient fuels in power plants; and increased the energy efficiency of our homes, industries, and businesses.

We know from history that fundamental change never comes easily or without a fight. But we're already seeing results. Just look at the facts: Since 2005, our emissions have fallen 6.5 percent, even as our economy continues to grow. What's more, we significantly scaled up our financial assistance to help developing countries mitigate and adapt to the effects of climate change.

We know we must do more, and believe me: we are. President Obama's Climate Action Plan will keep the United States on track to reach our goal of reducing U.S. greenhouse gas emissions in the range of 17 percent below 2005 levels by 2020. Commitments like this are an important signal to the world that America is ready to act.

This is a test of our leadership in the century ahead. We are not just the "indispensable nation"—today we must be the indispensable stewards of our shared planet. Strong, transparent action from all countries contributing to climate change is necessary to solve the global climate challenge. I am pleased to present this report, which demonstrates this Administration's commitment to leading the fight to confront climate change head-on, for our children and generations to come.

To read the 2014 Climate Action Report in its entirety, go to:
http://www.state.gov/documents/organization/219038.pdf.

CHAPTER NOTES

Chapter 1. "Out of Sight, Out of Mind"

1. The Center for Climate and Security, "Climate Security 101," February 2015, https://climateandsecurity.files.wordpress.com/2012/04/climate-security-101-2_21_15.pdf.

2. Zachary Davies Boren, "There are officially more mobile devices than people in the world," *The Independent*, October 7, 2014, http://www.independent.co.uk/life-style/gadgets-and-tech/news/there-are-officially-more-mobile-devices-than-people-in-the-world-9780518.html.

3. Eric Yosomono, J. Wisniewski, Ivan Farkas, Hillery Alley, "5 Byproducts of Modern Life That Are Burying Us in Garbage," Cracked.com, March 21, 2014, http://www.cracked.com/article_20885_5-byproducts-modern-life-that-are-burying-us-in-garbage.html.

4. *Municipal Solid Waste Generation, Recycling, and Disposal in the United States: Facts and Figures for 2012*, accessed May 13, 2015, http://www.epa.gov/solidwaste/nonhaz/municipal/pubs/2012_msw_fs.pdf.

5. "Overview of Greenhouse Gases," US Environmental Protection Agency, last modified May 7, 2015, http://epa.gov/climatechange/ghgemissions/gases/ch4.html; "Reducing Waste Can Make a Difference," US Environmental Protection Agency, accessed May 15, 2015, http://epa.gov/oppeoee1/climatechange/wycd/waste/downloads/cc-waste.pdf.

6. US Department of State, *United States Climate Action Report 2014*, 13, accessed June 21, 2015, http://www.state.gov/documents/organization/219038.pdf.

7. "Landfills," US Environmental Protection Agency, accessed May 15, 2015, http://www.epa.gov/solidwaste/nonhaz/municipal/landfill.htm.

8. Diane Cherry, *IEI Newsletter*, January 8, 2015, http://iei.ncsu.edu/wp-content/uploads/2015/03/Jan2015_Environments.pdf.

Chapter 2. Who Recycles

1. PR Newswire, "Global Recovered Paper Demand To Grow 2.5% Per Year Until 2029 As Trade Shifts Worldwide," Press Release, December 17, 2014, http://www.prnewswire.com/news-releases/global-recovered-paper-demand-to-grow-25-per-year-until-2029-as-trade-shifts-worldwide-300010687.html.

2. Christine Woodside, "Will Seattle Be the First U.S. City to Recycle Everything?" NextCity.org, September 4, 2014, https://nextcity.org/daily/entry/seattle-recycling-compost-sustainable-culture.

Chapter 3. Processing Recyclables

1. RISI, "2014 North American Pulp and Paper Mill Map," accessed May 18, 2015, http://www.risiinfo.com/risi-store/do/product/detail/2014_north_american_pulp_and_paper_mill_map.html.

2. Glass Packaging Institute, "Recycling," accessed June 18, 2015, http://www.gpi.org/recycling/glass-recycling-facts.

3. Alcoa, "Earn Cash Recycling," Alcoa.com, accessed June 18, 2015, http://www.alcoa.com/recycling/en/info_page/earn_cash.asp.

4. Elgin Recycling, "Recycling Facts," accessed May 19, 2015, http://www.elginrecycling.com/environmental/recycling-facts/.

5. Can Manufacturers Institute, "Recycling Facts," CanCentral.com, accessed May 19, 2015, http://www.cancentral.com/recycling-sustainability/facts.

Chapter 4. Metal Mines Above Ground

1. Steel Recycling Institute, *2013 Steel Recycling Rates*, http://www.recycle-steel.org/~/media/Files/SRI/Releases/Steel%20Recycling%20Rates%20Sheet.pdf.

2. The Aluminum Association, "Recycling," accessed May 25, 2015, http://www.aluminum.org/industries/production/recycling.

3. Copper Development Association, "Copper—The World's Most Reusable Resource," Copper.org, accessed May 25, 2015, http://www.copper.org/environment/lifecycle/g_recycl.html (May 25, 2015).

4. Mark Carpenter, "New Study Shows Strong Economic Impact of the U.S. Scrap Recycling Industry," Isri.org, May 21, 2015, http://www.isri.org/news-publications/article/2015/05/21/new-study-shows-strong-economic-impact-of-the-u.s.-scrap-recycling-industry#.VYQmBobvK1k.

5. "What Scrap Metal Yards Need to Do about PCBs," US Environmental Protection Agency, accessed May 25, 2015, http://yosemite.epa.gov/R10/OWCM.NSF/d60e13abe847c4cb882564de0071f735/c9fc199be44035a5882572ac007f368f!OpenDocument.

Chapter 5. Waste Becomes Energy

1. ecomaine, accessed May 22, 2015, http://www.ecomaine.org.

2. Timothy Williams, "Garbage Incinerators Make Comeback, Kindling Both Garbage and Debate," NYTimes.com, January 10, 2015, http://www.nytimes.com/2015/01/11/us/garbage-incinerators-make-comeback-kindling-both-garbage-and-debate.html?_r=0.

3. Brian Clark Howard, "How Cities Compost Mountains of Food Waste," News.NationalGeorgraphic.com, June 18, 2013, http://news.nationalgeographic.com/news/2013/06/130618-food-waste-composting-nyc-san-francisco/.

4. "NYC Organics Collection," NYC Department of Sanitation, accessed May 26, 2015, http://www1.nyc.gov/site/dsny/resources/initiatives/nyc-organics-collection.page.

5. Chris Nicholson, "NYC Schools Kick Organic Waste from Curb to Composting," DistrictAdministration.com, September 2014, http://www.districtadministration.com/article/nyc-schools-kick-organic-waste-curb-composting.

6. "Recycling Used Oil Saves Energy, Protects the Environment," American Petroleum Institute, accessed May 26, 2015, http://www.api.org/oil-and-natural-gas-overview/fuels-and-refining/engine-oil/recycling_used_oil_saves_energy.

7. American Petroleum Institute, "Used Motor Oil Collection and Recycling," RecycleOil.org, accessed May 26, 2015, http://www.recycleoil.org/more.html.

8. Earth911, "Used Motor Oil & Filters," accessed May 26, 2015, http://www.earth911.com/recycling-guide/how-to-recycle-motor-oil-and-filters/.

9. "Used Motor Oil," Davis, California, accessed May 26, 2015, http://recycling.cityofdavis.org/hazardous-waste/used-motor-oil.

10. Marc Lallanilla, "Tire Recycling: Let's Burn Some Rubber," GreenLiving.about.com, accessed May 26, 2015, http://greenliving.about.com/od/recyclingwaste/a/Tire-Recycling-Tyre-Recycling.htm.

11. "Tire Derived Fuel (TDF)," *Scrap Tire News*, accessed May 27, 2015, http://www.scraptirenews.com/tdf.php.

12. "Tire-Derived Fuel," US Environmental Protection Agency, May 27, 2015, http://www.epa.gov/osw/conserve/materials/tires/tdf.htm.

Chapter 6. Explosion of Plastics

1. Lynn Hasselberger, "22 Facts About Plastic Pollution (And 10 Things We Can Do About It)," *EcoWatch*, April 7, 2014, http://ecowatch.com/2014/04/07/22-facts-plastic-pollution-10-things-can-do-about-it/.

2. Laura Parker, "Eight Million Tons of Plastic Dumped in Ocean Every Year," News.NationalGeographic.com, February 13, 2015, http://news.nationalgeographic.com/news/2015/02/150212-ocean-debris-plastic-garbage-patches-science/.

3. Earth Talk, "Do Plastic Bags Ever Decompose?" IndyWeek.com, accessed Jun 4, 2015, http://www.indyweek.com/indyweek/do-plastic-bags-ever-decompose/Content?oid=1739045.

4. Eureka! Recycling, "Plastics in Depth: Recycling, Disposal, Toxicity, Health Impacts, and More," EurekaRecycling.org, last modified February 2014, http://www.eurekarecycling.org/page.cfm?ContentID=126.

5. Matthew Daneman, "More Cities Ban Polystyrene Foam, Citing Environment," USAToday.com, December 21, 2013, http://www.usatoday.com/story/news/nation/2013/12/21/polystyrene-foam-ban/4141735/.

6. Dow Chemical Company, "Dow Co-Sponsors 'Energy Bag' Pilot Program for Plastic Waste," Dow.com, February 17, 2015, http://www.dow.com/packaging/news-events/2015/20150217a.htm.

Chapter 7. Hazardous and Toxic Wastes

1. "A Citizen's Guide to the Superfund Program," US Environmental Protection Agency, accessed June 7, 2015, http://www.epa.gov/reg3hwmd/super/guide.htm.

2. "Lowry Landfill," US Environmental Protection Agency, accessed June 7, 2015, www2.epa.gov/region8/lowry-landfill.

3. Union of Concerned Scientists, "Coal Power: Air Pollution," UCSUSA.org, accessed June 8, 2015, http://www.ucsusa.org/clean_energy/coalvswind/c02c.html#.VXWgVEbvK1k.

4. Environmental Protection Agency, "Sources of Greenhouse Gas Emissions," EPA.gov, last modified May 7, 2015, http://epa.gov/climatechange/ghgemissions/sources/industry.html.

5. Lisa Song and David Hasemyer, "After Years of Inaction, EPA Tightens Toxic Air Standard for Oil Refineries," InsideClimateNews.com, April 22, 2015, http://www.insideclimatenews.org/news/22042015/after-inaction-epa-tightens-toxic-emissions-standard-oil-refineries?gclid=CMKo6fWigMYCFUsXHwod-SQAlw.

6. Environmental Protection Agency, *Citizen's Guide to In Situ Chemical Reduction*, accessed June 9, 2015, http://clu-in.org/download/citizens/vitrification.pdf.

7. David Rothbard, "Nanowires Help Bacteria Clean Up Toxic Waste," CFact.org, April 25, 2013, http://www.cfact.org/2013/04/25/nanowires-help-bacteria-clean-up-toxic-waste/#sthash.Srvq5Zqo.dpuf.

8. Susan Rush and Matt Drange, "Cleanup of Silicon Valley Superfund Site Takes Environmental Toll," CIROnline.org, March 17, 2014, http://cironline.org/reports/cleanup-silicon-valley-superfund-site-takes-environmental-toll-6149.

9. Greenpeace, "Stepping Lightly on the Earth: Everyone's Guide to Toxics in the Home," 1988, http://infohouse.p2ric.org/ref/33/32396.pdf.

Chapter 8. Nuclear Power and Waste

1. US Energy Information Administration, "Frequently Asked Questions," accessed June 9, 2015, http://www.eia.gov/tools/faqs/faq.cfm?id=207&t=3.

2. "What is Nuclear Waste?" WhatIsNuclear.com, accessed June 9, 2015, http://whatisnuclear.com/articles/waste.html#howmuch.

3. David Lochbaum, *The NRC and Nuclear Power Plant Safety in 2014* (Cambridge, Mass: Union of Concerned Scientists, 2015), 46, http://www.ucsusa.org/sites/default/files/attach/2015/03/nrc-2014-full-report.pdf.

4. Jefferson Lab, "Units of Measurement," accessed June 10, 2015, https://www.jlab.org/div_dept/train/rad_guide/fund.html.

5. US Department of Energy, "WIPP Update," WIPP.Energy.gov, June 11, 2015, http://www.wipp.energy.gov/wipprecovery/recovery.html.

6. Office of Environmental Management, "About Us," accessed June 11, 2015, http://energy.gov/em/about-us.

7. Office of Environmental Management, "Active Sites Additional Information," accessed June 11, 2015, http://energy.gov/em/cleanup-sites/active-sites-additional-information.

8. Valerie Brown, "Hanford Nuclear Waste Cleanup Plant May Be Too Dangerous," ScientificAmerican.com, May 9, 2013, http://www.scientificamerican.com/article/hanford-nuclear-cleanup-problems/.

9. Jeff Tollofson, "Safety Review for Yucca Mountain Site Released," Nature.com, January 29, 2015, http://www.nature.com/news/safety-review-for-yucca-mountain-site-released-1.16823.

Chapter 9. Help Save Our Planet

1. Blue Planet Prize Laureates, *Environment and Development Challenges: The Imperative to Act*, 7, accessed June 20, 2015, http://www.af-info.or.jp/en/bpplaureates/doc/2012jp_fp_en.pdf.

2. "IPCC WGII AR5 Summary for Policymakers," accessed June 13, 2015, https://ipcc-wg2.gov/AR5/images/uploads/IPCC_WG2AR5_SPM_Approved.pdf.

3. John F. Kerry, *United States Climate Action Report 2014*, 1, accessed June 13, 2015, http://www.state.gov/documents/organization/219038.pdf.

4. David O'Reilly, "Rabbis Issue a Letter on Climate Change," *Philadelphia Inquirer*, June 14, 2015, http://www.philly.com/philly/news/nation_world/20150614_Rabbis_issue_a_letter_on_climate_change.html.

5. The Shalom Center, "A Rabbinic Letter on the Climate Crisis," accessed June 16, 2015, https://theshalomcenter.org/civicrm/petition/sign?sid=17.

6. Pope Francis, Encyclical Letter Laudato Si' of the Holy Father Francis on Care for Our Common Home, accessed June 16, 2015, http://i1.cdn.turner.com/cnn/2015/images/06/18/papafrancesco_20150524_enciclica-laudato-si_en.pdf.

7. Katie Glueck, "Jeb Bush Knocks Pope on Climate Change Push," *Politico.com*, June 16, 2015 http://www.politico.com/story/2015/06/jeb-bush-knocks-pope-on-climate-change-push-119084.html.

8. Daniel Burke, "Pope Francis: 'Revolution' Needed to Combat Climate Change," CNN.com, June 18, 2015, http://www.cnn.com/2015/06/18/world/pope-francis-climate-technology-encyclical/index.html.

9. "Energy, Climate Change, and Our Environment," The White House, accessed June 13, 2015, https://www.whitehouse.gov/energy/climate-change.

10. Eco-Cycle, "Be Straw Free Campaign," accessed June 10, 2014, http://www.ecocycle.org/bestrawfree.

11. Vanessa Black, "14-Year-Old 'Kid Warrior' Rallies Youth Around the World to Protect the Planet," Ecowatch.com, April 22, 2015, http://ecowatch.com/2015/04/22/kid-warrior-xiuhtezcatl-martinez/.

12. Earth Guardians, "Itzcuauhtli Martinez," accessed June 15, 2015, http://www.earthguardians.org/itzcuauhtli/.

13. Dana Gunders, "Wasted: How America Is Losing Up to 40 Percent of Its Food from Farm to Fork to Landfill," NRDC Issue Paper, NRDC.org, August 2012, 4, http://www.nrdc.org/food/files/wasted-food-ip.pdf.

14. Ibid., 12.

15. "50 Ways to Help the Planet," accessed July 5, 2015, www.50waystohelp.com.

16. Youth Empowered Action, "Testimonials," accessed July 5, 2015, yeacamp .org/?page_id=55.

GLOSSARY

acid rain—Wet or dry deposits of acidic substances.

biodegradable—The property of a substance that allows microorganisms to break it down into simple, stable compounds.

carcinogen—A cancer-causing substance.

chlorofluorocarbons (CFCs)—Chlorine-based gas compounds used in refrigeration, as propellants, and in the manufacture of foam materials.

composting—Creating an environment for food scraps, yard wastes, and similar materials to decay into fertile humus.

conservation—The wise use of natural resources to reduce waste and loss.

cullet—Crushed glass.

dioxins—A group of chemical compounds that form during manufacturing processes or incineration of various waste products. Some dioxins are extremely toxic and carcinogenic.

dump—An uncontrolled site for disposing of waste now banned in most areas.

ferrous scrap—Scrap metal materials that contain iron or steel.

fission—The process of splitting into parts; in a nuclear reaction, an atom fissions or splits into fragments.

half-life—The time it takes for a radioactive substance to lose 50 percent of its activity.

hazardous waste—Waste that is toxic or explosive, can burn easily, or dissolves metal or flesh; such waste causes environmental and human health problems.

high-density polyethylene (HDPE)—A type of plastic resin used primarily to make milk jugs and bases of large soft drink containers.

humus—Soil from decayed vegetable matter that provides valuable nutrients for plants.

incinerator—A waste burner.

leachate—Any liquid and components within it that drain from a landfill or other site where people have placed materials.

leaching—The removal of various substances as water moves through soil.

low-density polyethylene (LDPE)–A type of plastic resin used to make film food wrap.

microbe—A minute organism.

nonferrous scrap—Scrap metal that does not contain iron or steel, such as aluminum, copper, lead, or nickel.

nuclear waste—Waste from nuclear weapons and power plants and a variety of products that contain radioactive materials.

organic—Waste from living organisms; usually refers to substances made up of vegetable or animal matter free from human-produced chemicals.

polychlorinated biphenyls (PCBs)—Heat-resistant compounds used in the manufacture of such products as fluorescent light fixtures and household appliances with electric capacitors.

polyethylene terephthalate (PET)—A type of plastic packaging material used for soda bottles.

plastic—A generic term for hundreds of different kinds of plastic materials.

photodegradable—Degrades or decomposes in sunlight.

pollute—To contaminate or make dirty by adding harmful substances.

polymer—A molecule made up of a long chain of units called monomers.

polystyrene foam—A plastic material used primarily for fast food containers, such as clamshells, cups, bowls, and trays.

radioactivity—The process by which atoms decay or change, emitting particles and rays.

polyvinyl chloride (PVC)—A type of plastic material used to make packaging products, such as blister packs and pour spouts for vegetable oils.

recycling—Reusing waste materials.

resin—A material used to make a liquid solid.

resource recovery—The process of accumulating large amounts of waste and burning it in a huge incinerator to produce energy.

sanitary landfill—A solid waste disposal site designed to reduce hazards to the environment and human health.

solid waste—Garbage that waste haulers dispose of in landfills.

Styrofoam—A trademarked polystyrene product of Dow Chemical.

toxic–Poisonous.

vitrification—The process of heating various materials to turn them into glass-like substances.

windrow—A row of leaves left to decompose.

FOR MORE INFORMATION

Earth Guardians
earthguardians.org
Encourages young people to take action and get involved to ensure the future of a sustainable planet.

Kids for Saving Earth
kidsforsavingearth.org
Educates, inspires, and empowers children to protect our environment.

Teens Turning Green
teensturninggreen.org
Devoted to education and advocacy around environmentally sustainable and socially responsible choices for individuals, schools, and communities.

DoSomething
dosomething.org
Provides young people with the tools to get involved in all aspects of social change.

FURTHER READING

Bily, Cynthia A., ed. *Garbage and Recycling*. Farmington Hills, MI: Greenhaven Press, 2013.

Fleischman, Paul. *Eyes Wide Open: Going Behind the Environmental Headlines*. Somerville, MA: Candlewick, 2014.

Humes, Edward. *Garbology: Our Dirty Love Affair with Trash*. New York: Avery, 2013.

Klein, Naomi. *This Changes Everything: Capitalism vs the Climate*. New York: Simon & Schuster, 2014.

Shaw, Randy. *The Activist's Handbook: Winning Social Change in the 21st Century* (second edition). Berkeley and Los Angeles, CA: University of California Press, 2013.

Thompson, Laurie Ann. *Be a Changemaker: How to Start Something That Matters*. New York: Simon Pulse, 2014.

INDEX